SALES DOMINATION

THE SMALL BUSINESS OWNER'S ULTIMATE GUIDE FOR CREATING SCALABLE SALES SYSTEMS

CLAY CLARK + JONATHAN KELLY

Sales Domination

ISBN 978-1-7342296-9-1

Copyright © 2021 by Clay Clark

Thrive Publishing

Published by Thrive Publishing
1100 Suite #100 Riverwalk Terrace
Jenks, OK 74037

Thrive Publishing books may be purchased for educational, business or sales promotional use. For more information, please email the Special Markets Department at info@ThriveTimeShow.com. For a good time visit ThriveTimeShow.com

CONTENTS

Chapter 1 7

IF YOU AREN'T GETTING RICH
DON'T B#%$, JUST IMPLEMENT THE
SUPER MOVES I USE

Chapter 2 25

THE THREE WAYS TO GET RICH AND
WHY IT'S MORE PAINFUL TO BE
POOR THAN REJECTED

Chapter 3 47

AT THE TOP EVERYONE CAN SELL

Chapter 4 79

WALKING ON HOT COALS,
MOTIVATIONAL SEMINARS, AND
INSPIRATIONAL TALKS ARE NOT
SALES TRAINING

Chapter 5 89

CUTTING THROUGH THE CLUTTER
OF COMMERCE

Chapter 6 103

YOU MUST AVOID PUFFERY
AT ALL COST

Chapter 7 107

YOU MUST GET THE LAW OF
CREDIBILITY TO WORK ON YOUR
BEHALF

Chapter 8 121

THE POWER OF PROOF
STATEMENTS

Chapter 9 129

CONSTRUCTING THE ULTIMATE
SCALABLE SALES SYSTEM

Chapter 10 135

DIAGRAM YOUR SALES PLAN

Chapter 11 159

THE ART OF THE COLD CALL +
LEARNING TO LOVE REJECTION

Chapter 12 181

EVEN WITH GREAT SALES
SYSTEMS, WITHOUT K.P.I.'S (KEY
PERFORMANCE INDICATORS) YOUR
SALES WILL DIE

Chapter 13 195

TRAINING GREAT SALESPEOPLE IS
NOT AN EVENT, IT'S A PROCESS

Chapter 14 199

COMMIT TO TAKING YOUR
COMMUNICATION SKILLS TO THE
NEXT LEVEL

Chapter 15 205

DETERMINE THE OTHER PROBLEMS
THAT YOU CAN SOLVE FOR YOUR
IDEAL AND LIKELY BUYERS THAT
NOW BOTH LIKE AND TRUST YOU

Chapter 16 213

HOW TO PROPERLY PRICE YOUR
PRODUCTS AND SERVICES

Chapter 17 219

DECLARE WAR ON THE
SALES-KILLING JARGON

Chapter 18 225

A CONVERSATION ABOUT LIFE
BEYOND JUST MOTIVATION

Chapter 19 231

DON'T COMPLICATE THE STRATEGY:
CALL THEM ALL UNTIL THEY CRY,
BUY OR DIE

Chapter 20 235

THE DREAM 100 SYSTEM CAN AND
WILL CHANGE YOUR LIFE!

Conclusion 241

THIS IS YOUR YEAR TO START
THRIVING AND TO MOVE BEYOND
JUST SURVIVING

CHAPTER 1

IF YOU AREN'T GETTING RICH DON'T B#%$, JUST IMPLEMENT THE SUPER MOVES I USE

WHEN YOU CAN'T SELL YOUR BUSINESS WILL GO TO HELL.

If you have a job as a salesperson and you can't sell, you will find yourself financially hurtin' and that is for certain. When you can't sell well, nothing goes well. And although money does not solve every problem, it does solve MOST problems. This book was written to teach you the specific proven sales strategies and systems that I have taught my clients time and time again to help them earn copious amounts of cash. This book was written to teach you how to DRAMATICALLY INCREASE YOUR INCOME so that you can experience both the financial and time freedom that can only be purchased with additional income.

WILL THIS SYSTEM WORK?

Yes. The system always works when it is applied to real businesses that sell real products and services to real people on the planet who are willing to actually buy the solutions, products and services that you or your organization sells.

WHY DO MY CLIENTS GROW BY 104% + ON AVERAGE WHEN 96% OF BUSINESSES FAIL WITHIN THE FIRST 10 YEARS ACCORDING TO INC. MAGAZINE?

First off, please don't blindly believe the claim that I have just made. Take the time to look over and investigate the clients listed below. These people listed below are my real clients who have really grown their businesses significantly.

FUN FACT
96% of Businesses Fail within 10 Years
https://www.inc.com/bill-carmody/why-96-of-businesses-fail-within-10-years.html

NOTABLE QUOTABLE:

"A feast is made for laughter, wine makes life merry, and money is the answer for everything."

ECCLESIASTES 10:19

FUN FACT
"78% of Workers Live Paycheck to Paycheck."
- Forbes
https://www.forbes.com/sites/zackfriedman/2019/01/11/live-paycheck-to-pay-check-government-shutdown/#761bcce34f10

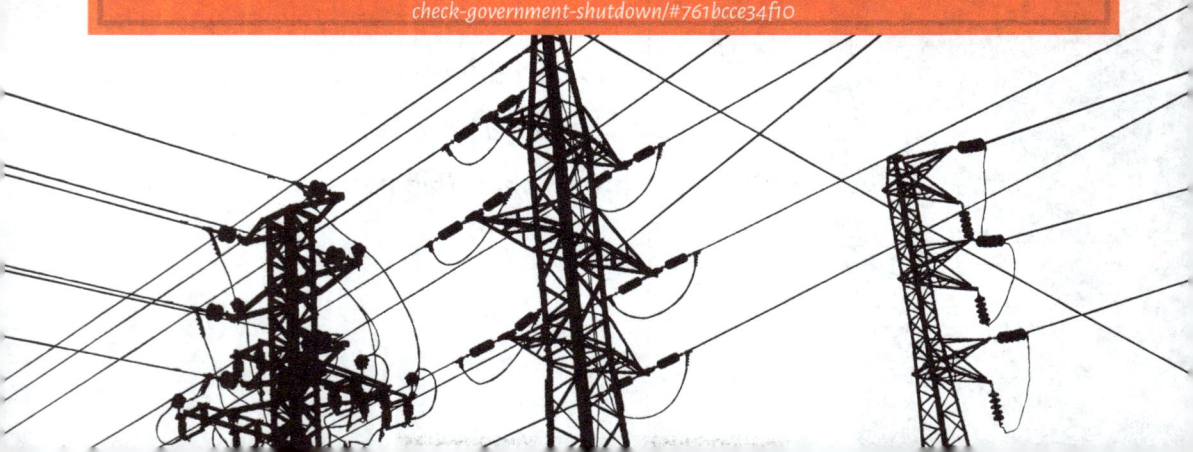

CIRCLE THE NEEDS / PROBLEMS THAT EARNING ADDITIONAL MONEY WOULD SOLVE FOR YOU:

* Your clothing needs.

* Your family's clothing needs.

* Your need to live in a nice home (when you live in the ghetto you experience ghetto drama caused by ghetto people having ghetto problems on a daily basis).

* Your vehicle needs repairs.

* Your need to pay off your student loans.

* Your need to buy health insurance.

* Your need to buy medical insurance.

* Your need to pay off medical bills.

CIRCLE THE FOLLOWING DREAMS THAT EARNING ADDITIONAL INCOME COULD TURN INTO REALITY FOR YOU:

* Your desire to send your kids to a better school.

* Your desire to send your kids to college.

* Your desire to hire a personal trainer or to buy a gym membership.

* Your desire to go out to eat more.

* Your desire to buy new furniture.

* Your desire to travel more.

* Your desire to upgrade your vehicle.

* Your desire to upgrade your home.

* Your desire to remodel your house.

* Your desire to buy a better bed.

* Your desire to buy a better television.

* Your desire to attend professional sporting events.

* Your desire to attend a great concert or show.

* Your desire to have that elective dental or cosmetic surgery you've always wanted.

* Your desire to pursue expensive and time-consuming hobbies (scuba diving, hunting, earning your pilot's license).

* Your desire to install a pool in your backyard.

* Your desire to install a hot tub in your backyard.

* Your desire to install a sauna in your backyard.

* Your desire to install a pool / billiard table in your home.

* Your desire to install a cryochamber in your home.

* Your desire to buy incredible surround sound speakers for your home.

* Your desire to build a woman cave or man cave in your home.

* Your desire to buy more crap that you want and don't need from the unholy triumvirate of retailers that I love buying things from (GuitarCenter.com, HobbyLobby.com, and Atwoods.com).

* Your desire to buy more silkie chickens.

THE SYSTEM ONLY WORKS IF YOU DO

IT'S SUPER SAD, BUT SUPER TRUE.

Most people living in these great United States and this land of opportunity waste a large portion of their lives trying to sell using strategies that will never work while also and never investing the time needed to learn to sell well. People get confused and stuck in a mental debate as to whether it is a scalable, linear, and learnable skill or whether it is a spiritual thing based upon the natural charismatic personality that a person is born with. My brother from another mother or my sister from another mister, I am here to teach you that sales is scalable, linear and learnable and that anybody who would tell you something different is 100% wrong.

IF YOU AREN'T ABLE TO SELL AT A HIGH LEVEL, IT IS BECAUSE YOU DON'T UNDERSTAND THE GAME.

Very few people on the planet understand the sales game and NEVER WILL because they are loyal to their dysfunction. Why is it that Dr. Zoellner and I have been able to build 16 multi-million dollar companies (thus far) between the two of us? Could it be that we know the proven sales systems and strategies that actually work? Look up just a few of the businesses that we have started and grown or have partnered with and ponder this question. Is sales trainable or are we just super lucky, talented, and natural born leaders?

* www.BankRegent.com (Sean Kouplen and Z bought this bank and grew it)

* www.DJconnection.com (I started this business)

* www.DRZoellner.com (Z started this business)

* www.EITRLounge.com (I started this business)

* www.EpicPhotos.com (I started this business)

* www.MakeYourLifeEpic.com (I started this business)

* www.PMHOKC.com (Randy Antrikan started this business and owns it and I have partnered with him in the city of Tulsa, Oklahoma)

* www.TipTopK9.com (Rachel and Ryan Wimpey started this company and I helped to scale and franchise it)

* www.Z66AA.com (Z started this business)

SALES IS A GAME THAT WE KEEP SCORE OF WITH DOLLARS AND CENTS

DECIDE THAT YOU CAN LEARN SALES AND THAT YOU WILL IMPLEMENT THE SALES SUPER MOVES TAUGHT IN THIS BOOK

DECIDE THAT YOU CAN LEARN SALES AND THAT YOU WILL IMPLEMENT THE SALES SUPER MOVES TAUGHT IN THIS BOOK

Decide today that you are going to implement the proven processes and sales strategies taught in this book. Knowledge without application is meaningless. You must decide that you are going to be done trying to get-rich-quick as a result of learning the newest sales hack, fad, and the newest motivational technique being taught by yet another charlatan who promises to teach you his "sales secrets" if you will just attend his next $4,000 magic money making conference.

NOTABLE QUOTABLE

"Remember, inspiration unused is merely entertainment. To get new results, you need to take new actions."

- DAVID BACH
(THE 9X *NEW YORK TIMES* BEST-SELLING AUTHOR, FINANCIAL EXPERT AND THRIVETIMESHOW.COM PODCAST GUEST)

This book has been written by me to help you without resorting to sharing inspirational stories, motivational allegories, and unreplicable spiritual stories about being in the right place at the right time. It's entirely possible for a dog to get super itself inspired enough to chase down a car. However, once the dog gets the car it doesn't know what to do with it. Most highly motivated sales people also doggedly chase down big potential clients and don't know what to even say when they are in front of their ideal and likely buyers. However, this book will teach you the super moves that you must use when you land that opportunity to present one-on-one face to face or one-on-one over the phone.

SALES SUCCESS IS NOT ABOUT MOTIVATION, IT'S ABOUT THE IMPLEMENTATION OF THE PROVEN SUPER MOVES

22

THIS BOOK IS A MANUAL, A HANDBOOK AND A PRACTICAL GUIDE FILLED WITH PROVEN, TRIED-AND-TRUE SUPER MOVES THAT I ENCOURAGE YOU TO USE.

Keep this book on your desk and use it often. Use this book as a reference guide. Take notes in the margin. Dog-ear the pages and make this your go-to book that you will use time and time again when you find yourself writing sales scripts and building sales workflows. This book does not have theory or opinions in it, because I have no patience for anything other than facts. This book will fill your mind with the facts, but it will be up to you to act.

A SPECIAL THANKS TO THE DILIGENT DOERS

I want to extend a big "thank you" to my diligent clients who have actually implemented the sales strategies that I use within my businesses and teach in this book. It was starting to get lonely at the top before you guys came along.

CHAPTER 2

THE THREE WAYS TO GET RICH AND WHY IT'S MORE PAINFUL TO BE POOR THAN REJECTED

ALTHOUGH I WILL TEACH YOU HOW TO GET RICH AS YOU READ THE PAGES OF THIS BOOK...

Know that if you live in the United States, you have a very small chance of getting rich by default (statistically speaking). Profits will get you rich, but wages will not. Thus, at some point you are going to need to either partner up with somebody or you are going to need to start your own profitable business.

HOW MANY PEOPLE LIVE IN THE UNITED STATES?

According to the most recent data that I can find, there are approximately 330,000,000 living in the United States as of 2019.

HOW MANY SMALL BUSINESSES ARE IN THE UNITED STATES?

According to an article published by *Forbes*, there are approximately 28,000,000 small businesses in the United States, and 22 million of them are self-employed with no additional employees (22 million "a dude and a truck" businesses).

https://www.forbes.com/sites/jasonnazar/2013/09/09/16-surprising-statistics-about-small-businesses/#1ae56e855ec8

WHAT PERCENTAGE OF BUSINESSES SUCCEED?

According to Inc. Magazine, 96% of businesses fail within 10 years.

https://www.inc.com/bill-carmody/why-96-of-businesses-fail-within-10-years.html

WHAT PERCENTAGE CHANCE DO YOU HAVE OF SUCCEEDING AS A SMALL BUSINESS OWNER IN THE UNITED STATES OF AMERICA (HOME OF THE WORLD'S BEST ECONOMY)?

If there are 28,000,000 million small businesses in a land filled with 330,000,000 people, that means that only 8% of the population is a small business owner. Just 4% of small businesses make it just 10 years, thus you have a .003% chance of succeeding. You don't have a 3% chance of succeeding. You don't have a 1/3 of a chance of succeeding. You have only a .0339% chance of succeeding by default!!! Thus, I think that it would be wise for you to take notes and commit yourself to diligently learning and apply the super moves that I am about to teach you.

IN THIS COUNTRY, THERE ARE THREE CONSISTENTLY PROVEN WAYS TO MAKE AN INCREDIBLE AND LIFE-CHANGING AMOUNT OF MONEY:

1) You can do work somewhere on the planet where very few others are willing to work:

* According to CNN Money, "Alaskan crewmen (crab fisherman) can earn up to $15,000 per month."

  https://money.cnn.com/2012/07/27/pf/jobs/crab-fishing-dangerous-jobs/index.htm

* According to CNN Money, "Oil rig workers make on average just under $100,000 a year, but salaries can vary widely depending on skills. It may be dangerous, difficult work, but oil drillers are well compensated for the job: The average salary for rig workers and other industry personnel was $99,175."

  https://money.cnn.com/2012/05/10/news/economy/oil_workers/index.htm

2) You can do work that nobody else has the ability to do:

* My client, Dr. Bryan Whitlock, is a highly-skilled surgeon who went to school for 16 years.

* My client, Colton Dixon, the hit song-writer and top 40 pop music artist, can sing like an angel and play the piano at an Elton John level.

3) You can do work that nobody else is willing to do (This is what I have always done):

* This is what I have always done. In order to get DJConnection.com to the top of the Google search engine results, I personally wrote the thousands of pages of original and keyword relevant text. To learn how to get to the top of the search engine results visit TheBestSEOBook.com.

* In route to building one of the most successful men's grooming lounges, we decided to offer to cut another man's hair for just $1 on their first service. And it costs us (all-in) nearly $23 to cut the man's hair that we are charging just $1 to cut. Why would we do that? We do this over and over again because this deal is SO HOT, SO GOOD and SO IRRESISTIBLE that it consistently drives in floods of potential new members to our grooming lounge each and every week. If you can experience a luxurious men's haircut experience for just $1, what do you have to lose?

In route to building one of the nation's most successful podcasts, (TheThrivetimeShow.com) I have written, recorded, edited, and launched over 2,000 shows. As a team, we have been rejected by well over 3,000 potential guests, and although we have succeeded in booking some of the most successful personalities in the world of business, I have been rejected time and time again. Below is a list just a few of the big-time guests that I have interviewed on the podcast over the years:

* Former CEO of YUM Brands (Pizza Hut, KFC, Taco Bell), David Novak

* Legendary Former Key Apple Employee Turned Venture Capitalist, Best Selling Author, Guy Kawasaki

* Senior Pastor of the Largest Church in America with Over 100,000 Weekly Attendees (Lifechurch.tv), Craig Groeschel

* 8x *New York Times* Best-Selling Author and Leadership Expert, John Maxwell

* Best-selling author and Pastor, John Bevere

* Celebrity Chef, Entrepreneur, and *New York Times* Best-Selling Author, Wolfgang Puck

* NBA Hall of Famer, David Robinson (2-time NBA Champion, 2-time Gold Medal Winner)

* *New York Times* Best-Selling Co-Author of *Rich Dad Poor Dad*, Sharon Lechter

* One of America's Most Trusted Financial Experts and Has Written Nine Consecutive *New York Times* bestsellers with 7 Million+ Books in Print, David Bach

* Senior Editor for *Forbes* and 3x Best-Selling Author, Zack O'Malley Greenburg

* Most Downloaded Business Podcaster of All-Time (EOFire. com), John Lee Dumas

* *New York Times* Best-Selling Author of *Purple Cow*, and former Yahoo! Vice President of Marketing, Seth Godin

* Co-Founder of the 700+ Employee Advertising Company (AdRoll), Adam Berke

* Emmy Award-winning Producer of the Today Show and *New York Times* Best-Selling Author of *Sh*tty Moms*, Mary Ann Zoellner

* *New York Times* Best-Selling Author of *Contagious: Why Things Catch On* and Wharton Business Professor, Jonah Berger

* *New York Times* Best-Selling Author of *Made to Stick* and Duke University Professor, Dan Heath

* International Best-Selling Author of *In Search of Excellence*, Tom Peters

* NBA Player and Coach, Muggsy Bogues (Shortest player to ever play in the league)

* NFL Running Back, Rashad Jennings (and Winner of Dancing with the Stars)

* Lee Cockerell (The former Executive Vice President of Walt Disney World who once managed 40,000 employees)

* Michael Levine (PR consultant of choice for Michael Jackson, Prince, Nike, Charlton Heston, Nancy Kerrigan, etc.)

* Billboard Contemporary Christian Top 40 Recording Artist, Colton Dixon

* *Conservative Talk Pundint, Frequent Fox News Contributor, Political Commentator and Best-Selling Author, Ben Shapiro*

SEE ADDITIONAL GUESTS AT THRIVETIMESHOW.COM/PODCAST

WHEN YOU LEARN HOW TO BECOME A SALES SUPERSTAR,

You will begin making copious amounts of cash because you can do work that nobody else is willing to do and you can do work that nobody else has the ability to do. During this book, I am going to destroy the delusional "woo-woo" sales tips that the world has been trying to fill your head with and I am going to replace that bogusness with best-practice sales tools and moves that you can use time and time again to close more deals and make more money.

FAST TALKING EGO MANIACS EXIT HERE

Unless a salesperson has been effectively trained, they typically attempt to compensate for their lack of sales skills with high-pressure, ego-filled, and patronizing half-truth, half-baked and high-pressure sales tomfoolery.

Think about that used car sales guy we've all had to deal with that is always obsessed with trying to convince that you that have to buy tonight or you will lose out on this "INCREDIBLE, ONCE-IN-LIFE-TIME" opportunity. This is why the average salesperson and business owner doesn't make much money and why buyers with an ounce of discernment and reasoning ability shut them down mercilessly every day, all day.

REDESIGN & REFRAME HOW YOU SELL

This book is about completely reframing and redesigning the way you think about sales, and how you attempt to sell. Remember most people are wrong about most things in the world of business by default which is why 96% of businesses fail within 10 years.

https://www.inc.com/bill-carmody/why-96-of-businesses-fail-within-10-years.html

IT'S ABOUT MECHANICS, LEARNABLE, AND REPEATABLE MOVES.

IT'S NOT ABOUT PERSONALITY

This book is filled with proven tactics and strategies, so you won't find any magic money get-rich-quick tips in the pages of this book. To succeed in the world of sales you don't need a ton of faith, you don't have to have ten years of experience in your industry, a belief in something larger than yourself, and I won't even require that you believe in yourself to master this system. All you have to do to win sales presentation after sales presentation is to implement the mechanics found in this book.

SALES IS THE HIGHEST PAID JOB ON THE PLANET AND YOU ARE GOING TO LOVE THIS BOOK!

You are going to love this book because it will change your life. Making money is fun. Winning in business is fun and nothing provides more continual inspiration than success. People that can sell well earn more money than any other profession on the planet. The leaders in our world of religion, politics, entertainment, business, leadership, and the arts can all sell well.

* **The Arts**
Justin Bieber performs to sold-out concerts.

* **Religion**
Bishop T.D. Jakes and Pastor Joel Osteen are best-selling authors.

* **Entertainment**
he prolific restaurateur, entrepreneur, and ThrivetimeSnow.com Podcast guest, Wolfgang Puck makes great food that is sold to millions of people.

* **Business**
My business partner and friend Jonathan Barnett is the founder of the OXIFresh.com franchise which now has sold over 400 locations.

* **Leadership**
The *New York Times* best-selling author of 84 books and the ThrivetimeShow.com Podcast guest, John Maxwell has sold 20 million books.

EVERYTHING HAS TO BE SOLD, EVEN FREE STUFF

Quit believing that sales does not matter and that you don't care about sales. If you can't sell your dreams and visions, everything will go to hell quickly. At some CRITICAL point during the epic careers of the names listed above, these people had to sell their ideas to the world. On this planet, even if you sincerely have a game-changing product or service that you want to provide to America or the world, you must know that you will not be able to help the world unless you know how to sell. If you can't sell your vision and ideas to the world, your gift to humanity, along with your freebies, will be rejected time and time again. You must deliver, package, and share your products and services the world, using a certain level of salesmanship, or the receiver of your products and services will not appreciate and grasp the true value of the gifts that you are offering.

15% OF PEOPLE IN THE WORLD MAKE ALL OF THE MONEY.

Everything on this planet has to be sold. However, very few humans on the planet sell successfully, thus people like me make 85% of the money. The next time your company organizes a sales meeting, look around and you will discover that of the 20 sales reps in the meeting, 3 of the salespeople will be making 85% of the money. Why are the top 15% of people dominating over and over again while the bottom 85% are losing so much and so often?

* Are the top 15% of salespeople lucky?

* Are the top 15% of salespeople born with a "good attitude for sales?"

* Are the top 15% of salespeople more charismatic?

* Are the top 15% of salespeople just "blessed" as we like to say in the midwest?

* Are the top 15% of salespeople "in the right place at the right time randomly"?

The top 15% of salespeople have learned and mastered the skill of effective sales. They fundamentally understand the transactional mechanics needed to sell well. The top 15% of salespeople know the proven process and best-practice sales moves that you are beginning to learn. People who are successful have learned how to become great verbal communicators and they have a high level of "emotional intelligence."

WHAT IS EMOTIONAL INTELLIGENCE?

NOTABLE QUOTABLE

"Emotional Intelligence is the ability to monitor one's own and other's emotions, to discriminate among them, and to use the information to guide one's thinking and actions."

DANIEL GOLEMAN
(THE *NEW YORK TIMES* BEST-SELLING AUTHOR AND INTERNATIONALLY RECOGNIZED PSYCHOLOGIST DANIEL GOLEMAN)

NOTABLE QUOTABLE

"If your emotional abilities aren't in hand, if you don't have self-awareness, if you are not able to manage your distressing emotions, if you can't have empathy and have effective relationships, then no matter how smart you are, you are not going to get very far."

DANIEL GOLEMAN
(THE *NEW YORK TIMES* BEST-SELLING AUTHOR AND INTERNATIONALLY RECOGNIZED PSYCHOLOGIST DANIEL GOLEMAN

NOTABLE QUOTABLE

"When dealing with people, remember you are not dealing with creatures of logic, but with creatures of emotion."

DALE CARNEGIE
(THE ICONIC COMMUNICATION EXPERT AND BEST-SELLING AUTHOR OF HOW TO WIN FRIENDS AND INFLUENCE PEOPLE)

YOU WERE TAUGHT AS A CHILD BY ALMOST EVERYONE

As a kid you were taught by the school system, professors and confused family members that if you will just go to school long enough, earn enough academic awards and degrees and work hard you will be destined for success. You were taught that with a college degree and a solid work ethic that eventually you would make your way to the top and that you would be able to earn enough money to drive luxury cars, to buy beautiful houses and to essentially turn the American dream into reality. However, I am telling you the hard truth: You have a .003% chance of succeeding. You don't have a 3% chance of succeeding. You don't have a 1/3 of a chance of succeeding. You have only a .0339% chance of succeeding by default!!!

CHAPTER 3

AT THE TOP EVERYONE CAN SELL

What your parents, teachers and well-meaning friends and family did not teach you is that as you get up closer to the top, you will see that at the top, EVERYONE CAN SELL WELL. WE CAN ALL SELL WELL. My friend, if you are going to reach your financial goals you are going to have to master your sales role. If you are the head of a big company you have to sell your team on:

* Coming to work with you

* Following checklists

* Implementing new systems

* Procedure changes

* Policy updates

* Price increases

* Visions for new projects

IN ORDER TO SUCCEED YOU MUST ALWAYS HAVE TWO SIMULTANEOUS PROFESSIONS

PROFESSION #1 - You must have a skill that pays the bills (machinists, doctor, lawyer, dentist, welder, search engine expert, basketball coach, cosmetic surgeon, etc.)

PROFESSION #2 - You must be a master of persuasion, influential conversation and sales.

Throughout your career you are going to have to constantly get better at your core profession (doctor, dentist, roofer, lawyer, etc.); however, these skills will be wasted and of no use to you or anybody else if you cannot sell the world on the benefits of using your products, skills, and services to solve their problems in exchange for the money that you seek.

YOU NEED TO BECOME A SICK FREAK WHO ACTUALLY LOVES TO SELL!

On this planet there are a few sick freaks who actually believe that selling is a blasty-blast and a ton of fun. My friend, I love selling. Oh selling is fun! However, inside most organizations, agencies and on college campuses the average person views selling as a dirty game and a necessary evil that no one wants to play. When people are transitioned to a sales position from an administrative position, some actually feel bad about it and a little shame about even telling people what they do for a living. Negative stories and tales of ill-prepared and rejection-adverse sales people are shared throughout entire departments and companies. And because 85% of people are not good at sales, if you ask the average person in your office or in your industry they almost all have endless stories of sorrow, poverty and rejection. However, I am here to share with you the gospel of wealth and stories of epic success.

YOUR LIFE DOESN'T HAVE TO BE POWERED BY POVERTY

I believe that you were not put on this Earth to be punished by poverty and that you don't have to endure a terrible existence during your time on this planet. I believe that your life was meant to be filled with fun, success, winning, and enjoyment as you reap the fruits of your diligent and disciplined work. Sales is super fun once you have learned and mastered the game. Persuading humans on this planet to take the actions that you want is a magnificently fun game. When you can sell well, you can afford to buy your time back. You can hire a dude to mow your lawn. You can order in your lunch. You can travel when you want to. You can buy silkie chickens when you want.

WHEN YOU CAN SELL WELL YOU CAN HAVE FUN ALONG THE JOURNEY TO MOUNT AWESOME

I am all about delayed gratification, living below my means and not living life without restraint like Antonio Brown or Dennis Rodman, but at the same time I want to have fun as I walk down the path up to the peak of financial success. Allow me to let me let you in on a quick secret...shhh...sales is fun once you have mastered the craft. So many books make sales seem like a terrible task, but if you can reframe it in your mind as a game, it gets more fun. And when you start viewing money as points it gets more fun. And when you start seeing yourself scoring an epic amount of points, now we are having a party.

I can remember when I was growing DJConnection.com, and for the first time our team booked 29 events in a single day.

That felt good. I remember the first time I built a multi-million dollar business that was fun. Soon, you too shall learn to love selling.

OUR CULTURE PICTURES SKILLED SALES PEOPLE AS DISHONEST, FAST-TALKING, DISORGANIZED AND SILVER-TONGUED DEVILS

However, top salespeople are 180 degrees opposite of this mental picture. The top salespeople on the planet are so incredible and so skilled that they don't ever even appear to be selling. The best salespeople on the planet are super detailed, prompt, unquestionably trust-worthy, diligent, funny (when they need to be) and kind. Top sales people earn their money.

MOST SALES PEOPLE DON'T UNDERSTAND THE TECHNICAL ASPECTS AND THE LINEAR PROCESS ONE MUST TAKE BUYERS THROUGH IN ORDER TO SUCCESSFULLY SELL

The average sales person is not good at sales because they have no idea how the flow of sales works. The winning combination for selling well is as follows:

* Step 1 - Rapport - You must establish rapport with your ideal and likely buyers.

* Step 2 - Needs - You must find the problems and needs of your ideal and likely buyers that you can solve.

* Step 3 - Benefits - You must clearly and powerfully be able to showcase what problems you can solve for your ideal and likely buyers and you must support all of the benefits that you deliver with facts. If you are unable to explain the problems that your company can solve and what you are selling to a nine-year-old child then you don't know what you are selling.

NOTABLE QUOTABLE

"If you can't explain it simply, you don't understand it well enough."

ALBERT EINSTEIN
(THE MAN WHOSE VAST KNOWLEDGE ALLOWED US TO CREATE MANHATTAN PROJECT AND THE WEAPONS NEEDED TO DEFEAT THE HATE-MONGERING-SATAN-INSPIRED-PRO-GENOCIDE AXIS POWERS WHICH INCLUDES NAZI GERMANY, ITALY, JAPAN AND THAT ASS-CLOWN AND MANIPULATIVE FASCIST LEADER ADOLF HILTER. MAY ADOLF BURN IN HELL.)

* Step 4 - Close - You must prompt your ideal and likely buyer to take action.

* Step 5 - Isolate Objections - You must be able to deal with the typical objections that presented by humans time and time again (no time, no need, no money) without being confrontational.

* Step 6 - Call to Action - You must be able to ask for the sale well after you have clearly presented your case and have explained why your product or service is worth your ideal and likely buyer spending their hard earned money with you.

Unfortunately, most sales people confuse talking at their prospect as persuasion. Because poor salespeople don't understand that selling successfully involves active listening and taking detailed notes based upon what your ideal and likely buyer is saying, they tend to talk over potential buyers.

SELLING IS ABOUT SOLVING PROBLEMS

At its core, sales is about solving problems for your ideal and likely buyers. Selling is not about hustling in a bombastic tone while watching The Wolf of Wall Street over and over for motivation. To sell well, you have to put down the Red Bull and listen attentively to what your ideal and likely buyers are saying. When you are perceived as being aggressive you will lose a lot of deals, if not all of the deals. Be persistent, but do not be aggressive when you are attempting to sell things to humans on this glorious planet Earth.

REMEMBER THAT YOU HAVE 2 EARS AND 1 MOUTH OR YOUR POTENTIAL DEALS WILL QUICKLY GO SOUTH

Most salespeople on the planet simply will not stop talking long enough to allow time for the buyer to explain their unique needs and wants. People's favorite topic is themselves, thus if you want to be liked by your ideal and likely buyer you must learn how to ask questions that will insure that the buyer will like you because they are talking 2 to 3 times more than you about their favorite topic (themselves and about solving problems for themselves).

IT'S OK TO LET THE BUYERS THINK

Poor sales people are afraid of any silence at all and thus they do not allow buyers to ever think. Poor sales people guess about the buyer's needs and then when they get it wrong they guess again and again until their potential deal explodes. Poor sales people guess about the buyers needs and they are almost always wrong. Then to make the situation worse bad sales people attempt to use dirty, old, and depreciated sales moves that they have learned from other high-pressure and bad sales people.

BUYERS WILL DO BATTLE WITH YOU ONCE THEY SMELL AN AGGRESSIVE SALES PITCH

Buyers are so often talked down to and talked at by bad sales people they have learned how to quickly shut down any attempt to "sell them." Soon the relationship between a potential buyer and an aggressive sales person becomes all out war. Buyers begin to view sales people as the enemy and they launch verbal grenades at these poor sales people in their attempt to blow up the conversation and to get them out of their face, out of their living room, or off of their phone.

The buyer knows all of the dirty tricks and they will begin to feel as though they are being scammed and caught in some joke where they are the punchline, and they will go off at bad sales people and act horribly hostile. Buyers view bad sales people as amateur hustling cockroaches that must be crushed or immediately rejected. If this describes your life as a sales person up to now, you may have found yourself going down the downward spiral of losing confidence and hope for a better future where your sales are not terrible. Soon you may begin going online to search for another job that is "easier" and "more fulfilling" and then you'll wake up one day and realize, "Holy crap! I'm not wealthy! What happened!?"

SO HOW TO PUSH PAST ALL OF THE PUSH-BACK PRESENTED BY YOUR IDEAL AND LIKELY BUYERS?

You must reframe how you view sales starting now. As a salesperson, your job exists for ONE REASON. Your job is to get your ideal and likely buyer to take action and make a commitment. Most salespeople do not ever even ask for the sale. This blows my mind! How is your ideal and likely buyer expected to ever buy something from you if they don't know what you are selling and you never ask for the deal. Are we expecting humanity to suddenly wake up in the middle of the night with a burning desire to pay us? If you don't ask for the sale you are wasting your time, the buyer's time, and you're going to be poor as a result of this mentality.

OUR CULTURE HAS STOPPED LISTENING

The culture we now live in has killed the listening skills of most people. As a highly-skilled salesperson you must learn to listen attentively and in a way that the vast majority of the population cannot relate to. We are now constantly bombarded by push notifications, missed calls, missed emails, mass mailers, billboards, text message marketing, Facebook updates, Facebook advertisements, Instagram updates, Youtube updates, Linkedin connection requests, job board updates, and countless other types of distracting digital clutter. In fact, consider these disturbing statistics:

FUN FACT

New Study Shows You're Wasting 21.8 hours a Week

The business leaders we polled spent 6.8 hours per week on low value business activities that they could easily have paid somebody else $50/hour or less to handle for them. They wasted 3.9 hours each week indulging in what we might call escapist "mental health breaks" --streaming YouTube videos and checking social media. They wasted 3.4 hours a week handling low-value emails and 3.2 hours a week dealing with low-value interruptions that easily could have been handled by somebody else on staff. They spent 1.8 hours a week handling low-value requests from co-workers and another 1.8 hours a week putting out preventable fires. Finally, they spent an average of 1 hour each week sitting in completely non-productive or wasteful meetings. Total that up and we're looking at 21.8 wasted hours each week -- hours that are going up in smoke while you're doing things that contribute little to no value to your company.

https://www.inc.com/david-finkel/new-study-shows-youre-wasting-218-hours-a-week.html

"Here's another disturbing stat: This tally seems to increase daily, but by one study's count, the typical smartphone user interacts with their phone around 85 times per day."

- Why Your Smartphone Is Destroying Your Life - Psychology Today - Anna Akbari Ph.D.- https://www.psychologytoday.com/us/blog/startup-your-life/201801/why-your-smartphone-is-destroying-your-life

"According to research cited in *Forbes*, the average office worker spends 2.5 hours a day reading and responding to an average of 200 emails, of which approximately 144 (mostly CCs and BCCs) aren't relevant to their job."

- The Average Worker Spends 51% of Each Workday on These 3 Unnecessary Tasks - Inc. Magazine
- Geoffrey James - https://www.inc.com/geoffrey-james/the-average-worker-spends-51-of-each-work-day-on-these-3-unnecessary-tasks.html

"Research published by the University of Chicago found that even if cell phones are turned off, turned face down or put away their mere presence reduces people's cognitive capacity." - Research continually shows how distracting cell phones are—so some schools want to ban them

- CNBC - Abigail Hess https://www.cnbc.com/2019/01/18/research-shows-that-cell-phones-distract-students--so-france-banned-them-in-school--.html#targetText=Research%20published%20by%20the%20University,presence%20reduces%20people's%20cognitive%20capacity.

When you are listening to your ideal and likely buyers you must listen to what is actually being said, all while resisting the temptation to interrupt them and to immediately share how your product or service can solve the problem. You also must learn to listen to what is not being said. You must get yourself so focused on your potential ideal and likely buyers that you pick up on their body language, their tone of voice, and everything that they are communicating without directly saying. To become a master salesperson, you must also learn how to pick up on what cannot be said due to internal politics, family dynamics and those situations that tend to make life "more complicated" that we would ideally like it to be.

WHEN LISTENING TO YOUR IDEAL AND LIKELY BUYERS, YOU MUST HOLD YOURSELF ACCOUNTABLE TO DOING THE FOLLOWING FOUR TASKS SIMULTANEOUSLY:

* You must devote 100% of your focus and attention to your ideal and likely buyer. You must not allow yourself to become distracted or preoccupied by anything (interruptions from your smartphone, people in your office, etc.). You must not ever interrupt your ideal and likely buyer, and you must never fill in the blanks when they talk in an attempt to make the conversation move on at a faster pace.

* You must commit yourself to providing extreme empathy to your ideal and likely buyer. You must be so committed to being focused on what they are saying that you are almost able to share their pains, their ups and their downs.

* Actively take notes. Whenever your ideal and likely buyer says anything you must mentally commit yourself to believing that what they are about to say is the most important thing that a human has ever said. As you listen to what they are saying, take notes and repeat back to them what was said often so that they know you are listening to them with your 100% full attention.

* As you listen, you must be writing down the solutions that you and your team are able to provide for your ideal and likely buyer without saying it until the appropriate time. Nobody likes to be interrupted and I know that you are excited about the problems that you can help your ideal and likely buyer to solve, yet you still must wait until the appropriate time to share the solutions that both you and your company can provide.

The world around us has all been designed to cater to the passive part of your brain that loves to unwind and slow down for entertainment. As we endlessly and aggressively search around the planet and the digital universe in search of entertainment, as a society, many people have simply lost the ability to listen attentively to the person we are supposed to be conversing with. By default, people no longer have the patience to listen to humans sharing their stories as we once did, before this massive world of constant digital distractions became prevalent. The entire lives of Steve Jobs (The co-founder of Apple), Thomas Edison (The founder of General Electric), and Ray Kroc (The founder of McDonald's) have been condensed into two hour documentaries or films "based on a true story", which means that the screenplay is generally 40%. Thus, the world we live in is quick to celebrate the life of P.T. Barnum, who the hit movie The Greatest Showman was made about without actually knowing about P.T. Barnum's real life and real character. The world loves the actor Hugh Jackman who played the role of P.T. Barnum, but the real P.T. Barnum was not a nice guy. In fact, he bought an elderly slave woman who was both blind and partially paralyzed and he displayed her at his Circus as being George Washington's wet nurse. P.T. Barnum also hired the "Bearded Lady" when she was just a kid to star in his famous "Freak Show."

In this world we live in, most people now simply passively watch and consume media and blindly accept that what they are watching is true. In today's culture most people don't listen and pay attention even when their income and financial success depends on it. With the advent of social media, we have now become a country filled with 300 million content creators (people with social media accounts). Everyone is now a self-proclaimed expert and very few actually take the time to listen to proven experts and their customers. Today, I went into a local grocery store / restaurant by

Braums and the clerk who was checking me out did not make eye contact and continued to talk into her headset to somebody else during our entire interaction. On Wednesday night of this week, I took my wife out to eat at a great Italian restaurant in Tulsa, Oklahoma and I briefly observed more than half of the people seated at the tables near to us looking at their phones and not the family and friends whom they were out to dinner with.

THE NOTETAKERS ARE THE MONEY MAKERS

Over the years I have been able to shadow and to spend massive amounts of time shadowing some of the top business leaders on the planet including: The founder of Hobby Lobby, the President of QuikTrip convenience stores, the founder of Skyy Vodka, George Foreman, etc. During these interactions, I was always blown away at how mentally present they were when they were physically present with me. According to research reported in the legendary salesbook, *Soft Selling in a Hard World* "In tests at the boardroom level, executives retained 90% of the information delivered in a 45-minute presentation. Assembly line workers retained 25%. Which came first: listening skills or promotion? Who knows? For the average person, improving listening skills is a reasonable ambition. You may never make the boardroom, but it may get you off the assembly line." - *Soft Selling in a Hard World - Jerry Vass*

THERE ARE NO NATURAL BORN SALESPEOPLE

Since I started my first business at the age of 16, I have run into business people who are bad at selling and fond of talking about how lucky such and such is to be a "born salesman." In fact, the people who are the worst at selling are generally the most emotionally committed to the idea of "the born salesman." I TRULY BELIEVE THAT THERE ARE AS MANY "BORN SALESMAN" AS THERE ARE "BORN OPHTHALMOLOGISTS AND BORN COSMETIC SURGEONS. Two of my incredible clients, Doctor Timothy Johnson (Ophthalmologist) and Dr. Bryan Whitlock (Cosmetic Surgeon) have worked incredibly hard to get to where they are today and I can tell you that Dr. Bryan Whitlock spent 16 years in school to earn the position that he now enjoys in life and Dr. Timothy Johnson had to diligently delay gratification for over a decade to enjoy the lifestyle he now lives.

Note: Learn more about the real success stories of Dr. Timothy Johnson and Dr. Bryan Whitlock by visiting:

* https://www.thrivetimeshow.com/business-podcasts/business-coach-case-study-the-15-growth-of-dr-timothy-johnson/
* https://www.ttowneyes.com/
* https://www.whitlockcosmetic.com/

In order to become successful you must stop believing and buying into the myth of "the born salesman" and you must embrace that the world's top salespeople sacrificed and learn the sales super moves that I am now teaching you.

FORMAL EDUCATION DOES NOT UNDERSTAND THE SALES VOCATION

Currently, the vast majority of formal education does not offer degrees in practical sales. You can go to college and earn a degree in marketing, but almost none of what you will be taught or what you will learn will actually ever translate into sales. Why? I hate to break it to you, but as a general rule the people who can't actually successfully market products and services rush to a college campus to become a professor who teaches a class about marketing and sales.

NOTABLE QUOTABLE

"University administrators are the equivalent of subprime mortgage brokers selling you a story that you should go into debt massively, that it's not a consumption decision, it's an investment decision. Actually, no, it's a bad consumption decision."

- PETER THIEL
(THE BILLIONAIRE INVESTOR WHO IS THE CO-FOUNDER OF PAYPAL, PALANTIR TECHNOLOGIES AND FOUNDERS FUND. HE WAS RANKED NO. 4 ON THE *FORBES* MIDAS LIST OF 2014, WITH A NET WORTH OF $2.5 BILLION IN 2018)

THE HARD SELL IS DEAD AND IS NEVER COMING BACK

The "hard selling" strategy has been taught by countless stock brokers and used car dealers. It has been celebrated in movies like, The Boiler Room and The Wolf of Wall Street, but yet it is still very, VERY dead. Buyers today are jaded, and hardened by the endless barrage of B.S. delivered by salespeople who are preying on consumers based upon their belief that common sense is no-longer common.

IT'S EASIER TO REJECT A HARD SELL

Buyers on the planet earth today have seen many failed attempts to be hard sold and thus they are now able to reject blatant attempts to be hard-sold with an ease and practiced comfort that is mind blowing and befuddeling to bad salespeople. Consumers today listen to anything that sounds bogus, scammy, insincere, and fake and then they fire up the rejection machine. If the wrong tone of voice is picked up or if the body language looks insincere, buyers today will shut you down. When you use doubtful words or portray a lack of confidence to your ideal and likely buyers today, you will get shut down.

DO YOU WANT THE GOOD NEWS OR THE BAD NEWS?

The good news is that most salespeople on the planet are terrible. The bad news is that by default most salespeople are terrible. However, we must remember that sales is a very trainable and transferable skill so you must now learn the new approach. When you invest the time to learn the systemic and mechanics of a successful sales presentation you will discover that you potential buyers will no longer aggressively attack you. In fact, they will befriend you. When you learn to implement the "soft-selling" super moves that I will teach you throughout this book, you will become great at knowing when to use your super powers when dealing with buyers who are responding to you with their typical "hard-sell responses."

LEARNING NEW HABITS

Once you learn to implement the super moves that I am teaching you within this book you will find yourself becoming a "Jedi" of sales and a person who has developed new habits. Once you have invested the time needed to create these new "sales habits" you will find that these habits are going to get out and do most of the work for you.

IT'S EASIER TO TEACH A NEW DOG NEW TRICKS

If you are the owner of a business you will soon discover that it is INFINITELY easier to teach these sales supermoves to a new salesperson than it is to teach these moves to a "used" and "high-mileage" salesperson who has "seen it all" and allegedly "done it all" while still applying for an entry level sales job at the age of 52. I have found it to be true time and time again when working with huge companies (Hewlett-Packard, Maytag University, UPS, Farmers Insurance, etc.) and small, that rapidly growing companies such as www.TipTopK9.com, www.FullPackageMedia.com and www.PMHOKC.com, these "new kids on the block" are easier to train than veteran salespeople who have either subconsciously or consciously committed themselves to being a dysfunctional sales destroyer.

CHAPTER 4

WALKING ON HOT COALS, MOTIVATIONAL SEMINARS, AND INSPIRATIONAL TALKS ARE NOT SALES TRAINING

Nothing is worse than working in or for an organization that has confused motivational and inspirational training with sales training.

Years ago I used to work with a muscular man fond of wearing super small shirts, underpaying (or not paying) his employees, and speaking entirely in generalities, vagaries, and visions. This only worked for him for so long. Although he had committed salespeople working for him that were 100% committed to his vision he never actually had a plan and every meeting he led was essentially a hype meeting filled with endless, empty, hollow, and motivational phrases like "if we can see it, we can believe it."

Although the phrase, "if you can conceive it, we can achieve it" may be of some value for entrepreneurs it didn't help his salespeople who did not know what words to say when the phone rang. Everyone he hired never had a call script to use when answering his phones before I was able to help him. For years, his potential customers would e-mail in with their frequently asked questions, he frequently (always) had a different answer, and would frequently (always) not find the time needed to document the best-practice responses to the frequently asked questions. And despite his personally intense work ethic, he chose to be mentally lazy, which is why he struggled for so long to retain his clients before I was able to help him. My friend, it is imperative that you do not confuse motivational training with sales training. Many people on the planet earth are sufficiently motivated to become doctors, but they need eight years of training, practicing and role-playing to become one. Don't think that you salespeople are going to be somehow able to master the skills that you are teaching them without rigorous and repetitive training. You must understand that it is not important that it is not important to practice until perfect, but it is important to practice until you can't get it wrong.

You simply cannot become one of the world's top sales professionals if you do not practice and practice until you cannot get it wrong. The more and more that you invest the time needed to practice the more attentive to your ideal and likely buyers you will become. This will then cause you to earn more money. I personally recommend that you practice by reading your sales script outloud for 30 minutes per day for the next 4 weeks and that you would listen to your call from the day before on your commute to work if possible (use ClarityVoice.com to make this possible). Do not ever underestimate the incredible value of consistent and diligent practice.

SALES IS A PROFESSION THAT MOST IDENTIFY WITH THE WORST OF THE PROFESSIONS

Because we live in a world where the top salespeople are not identified as actually being good at sales, thus when we think about sales we usually only think about the worst salespeople. The best salespeople in the world are so skilled and masterful at their craft that we as a culture don't even recognize when they are selling. However, when you take the time needed to analyze sales moves that the world's best salespeople, business leaders, presenters, pastors, politicians, and media personalities use you will soon discover that they are using the mechanical, repeatable and learnable sales moves that I will teach you ALL-OF-THE-TIME. In fact, they never turn it off when they are in public and in front of others, thus we as a culture chalk it up to them having a "great personality."

DO YOU BELIEVE THESE PEOPLE LEARNED SALES OR DO YOU THINK THAT THEY WERE BORN WITH THE SKILLS?

NOTABLE QUOTABLE

"Somebody once said that the chains of habits are too light to be felt until they are too heavy to be broken. I had been terrified of public speaking. I couldn't do it. I'd thrown up. And I knew that if I didn't cure it then I would never cure it. So I saw an ad in the paper for the Dale Carnegie course which worked on your ability to speak in public. If I hadn't done that my whole life would be different. So in my office you will not see the degree I got from the University of Nebraska. You will not see the master's degree that I got from Colombia University, but you will see the little award certificate I got from the Dale Carnegie course."

WARREN BUFFETT

(THE FAMOUS "ORACLE FROM OMAHA" AND ARGUABLY THE MOST SUCCESSFUL INVESTOR OF ALL-TIME WHO IS WORTH $87.3 BILLION DESPITE HAVING GIVEN AWAY $36 BILLION SINCE 2000. TO PUT THAT IN CONTEXT AS OF 2020, ELON MUSK IS REPORTED TO BE WORTH APPROXIMATELY $32 BILLION AS OF JANUARY 25TH, 2020.)

I personally know many SUPER SUCCESSFUL people and I have interviewed nearly 1,000 SUPER SUCCESSFUL people on our www.ThrivetimeShow.com podcast, and I can tell you that ALL OF THEM are great at sales. What I can't tell you is how much of their skill is learned versus how much is just the natural talent that they were born with. However, in the United States we celebrate and heavily financially compensate those that have the power to motivate a room, solve problems, convince a buyer, move ideas across the cultural landscape, inspire change, and those who can sell well. I can also tell you that the OVERWHELMING MAJORITY of the SUPER SUCCESSFUL that I have interviewed have told me that they have read and applied the principles found within How to Win Friends and Influence People by Dale Carnegie and Think and Grow Rich by Napoleon Hill. Thus, I would highly recommend for you to read these two books as well.

CHAPTER 5
CUTTING THROUGH THE CLUTTER OF COMMERCE

Most of you reading this book have a smartphone, a television and you typically drive or commute to work in some capacity. While on the way to work you are going to be bombarded with thousands of messages throughout your day. As potential buyers, we have learned how to survive this information overload by simply refusing to acknowledge the presence of these distractions, interruptions and attempts to steal a moment of our time.

With the industrial revolution and mass production came the concept of selling to the masses. Up until this time in American history, selling was done in a more personal way. When you wanted to buy something you would go to Mr. Jones' Local Grocery Store which was owned and operated by Mr. Jones who you knew from church. Back in the day you were buying your butter, milk and eggs you needed from Mr. Jones (somebody you knew). However, today as a result of mass-production, salespeople have a lot of stuff to sell to their ideal and likely buyers. Thus, a new job title was created and a new professional was invented. This profession is that of being a salesperson.

HOW TO STAND OUT WHEN THE BRAINS OF CONSUMERS ARE BEING BOMBARDED WITH RELENTLESS MARKETING MESSAGES

In order to help the salesperson to generate leads businesses began to market to their ideal and likely buyers with newspaper advertising, radio commercials, television advertising, billboard advertising, and TV pitchmen. As result when you and I think of salesman now we mentally picture:

* George Foreman and his Lean Mean Grill Machine

* Billy Blanks and his Tae Bo products

* Ron Popeil and his latest greatest invention ranging from his Chop-O-Matic hand food processor, to his Beef Jerky Machine and his legendary Spray-On Hair.

* Vince Offer and his "ShamWow" products

* Billy Mays and his Mighty Putty, Hercules Hook, the Awesome Auger and more...

* The local car dealership owner pitching his latest special

However, I want to encourage you to develop a different mental picture in your mind when you begin to think of selling. When you think of selling (influencing) moving forward I would invite you to picture in your mind the following people:

* Steve Jobs - (As the co-founder of Apple and the former CEO of PIXAR Steve Jobs was incredible at convincing his employees to believe that they had both the capacity and tenacity needed to create "insanely great products." He also had developed the communication skills needed to convince the world that the newest product that he was releasing was a product that solved so many problems for you that you simply could not live without it (The personal computer, the iPod, iTunes, the iPhone, the iPad, etc.). During Steve's time on the planet, he was the world's greatest technology salesman.

* Oprah Winfrey - (Oprah is the world's most well known media personality. She is a media executive, an actress, a talk show host, a television producer, a philanthropist and much, much more. During her time on the planet she has sold you (influenced you) on joining her book club and buying the books she recommends, drinking the Starbucks beverages named after her and to see the films that she has chosen to act in. Whether you want to label her as the world's best media salesperson, or one of the most influential people on the planet it really doesn't matter. Oprah is a master saleswoman.)

* Thomas Edison – (As the founder of General Electric and the creator of the first commercially viable lightbulb, recorded audio, recorded sound and 1,093 patents he sold America on the idea that you could not live without his lightbulb, his Edison phonograph (record player) and countless other GE products. During his time he was the world's greatest salesman.)

* Bishop T.D. Jakes – (Bishop T.D. Jakes is the man I listen to each and every morning on my way to work and he is the senior pastor of The Potter's House, which is a non-denominational megachurch located within Dallas, Texas. He is a best-selling author, a real estate developer, and a successful entrepreneur. Every Sunday he masterfully sells the gospel and the benefits of becoming a committed follower of Christ.)

In this world of perpetual distraction and mass marketing it is increasingly important for you to master your sales skills so that you, your product or service and your company does not go unnoticed, unpurchased and out of business.

FUN FACT:

Did you know that according to Nielsen, the average American adult now spends 11 hours per day interacting with media?

- https://www.nielsen.com/us/en/insights/article/2018/time-flies-us-adults-now-spend-nearly-half-a-day-interacting-with-media

IN OUR CULTURE TODAY, BUYERS ARE READY TO BE ATTACKED AND TO REJECT BAD SALESPEOPLE

In our world today, buyers essentially believe that they are always under attack and sellers believe that they are on the attack. However, there still is a proven method for selling well in a world that has learned to quickly reject the attempts of salespeople who are attempting to sell to the masses.

If you are willing to invest the time needed to create a carefully crafted sales script based upon the sales super moves that I will teach you on the following pages you will make a lot of money as long as you are selling a real product or service to real people on the planet who are really willing to exchange their hard-earned money for the real solutions that you really provide. The technique and the moves that I am going to teach you are known as soft-selling.

YOU MUST BELIEVE IN YOUR PRODUCT

Don't over spiritualize this or overthink this, but you must actually believe in the products and services that you are selling and the solutions that they provide to your ideal and likely buyers in able to sell it well. In fact, you must believe in the solutions that you and/or your business provides to your ideal and likely buyers so much so that would be easily able to carefully craft a multi-million dollar 60-second Super Bowl commercial that would convince 50 million people at one time to check out the products and service that you are offering.

Now take a moment and actually write down the 60-second Super Bowl commercial that would convince 50 million people at one time to check out the products and services that you are offering on the lines below:

_____

_____

_____

_____

_____

_____

_____

_____

_____

_____

_____

_____

_____

_____

_____

WHY WAS THIS EXERCISE SO HARD TO DO?

In order to sell well on the planet earth, you must become great at writing sales pitches that follow the following format (as mentioned earlier):

* Step 1 - Rapport - You must establish rapport with your ideal and likely buyers.

* Step 2 - Needs - You must find the problems and needs of your ideal and likely buyers that you can solve.

* Step 3 - Benefits - You must clearly and powerfully be able to showcase what problems you can solve for your ideal and likely buyers and you must support all of the benefits that you deliver with facts.

* Step 4 - Close - You must prompt your ideal and likely buyer to take action.

* Step 5 - Isolate Objections - You must be able to deal with the typical objections that presented by humans time and time again (no time, no need, no money) with being confrontational.

* Step 6 - Call to Action - You must be able to ask for the sale well after you have clearly presented your case and have explained why your product or service is worth your ideal and likely buyer spending their hard earned money with you. Based upon years of experience coaching both huge and small brands, I recommend using an incremental close that looks and sounds something like this:

1. Based upon what we've talked about, which package looks the best for you and your business at this point?

2. When ideally would you like to start?

3. Did you want to pay your deposit via a debit or credit card?

4. What are the numbers on the card, what's the cvv code and the expiration date?

5. What is the zip code associated with the credit card?

6. Great, so we will charge you $ _____ on _____ (day).

7. And what email address do you want me to send you the receipt to?

YOU MUST LEARN TO PUT YOURSELF IN THE PERSPECTIVE OF YOUR IDEAL AND LIKELY BUYERS AT ALL TIMES:

When most of your ideal and likely buyers are sitting face-to-face with you in your office or they are listening to you over the phone they are always asking themselves:

* *"Why should I care?"*

* *"How can I benefit from this?"*

* *"How can you prove that what you are saying is true?"*

In order to have a realistic opportunity to sell the products and services that you offer to ideal and likely buyers that will actually appreciate the solutions that you and your company can provide it is critically important that you invest the time right now needed to define who your ideal and likely buyers actually are:

From the list below, circle which marketing vehicles that you think are most likely to carry your marketing message effectively to your ideal and likely buyers:

Adwords

Amazon.com

Automobile Wraps

Billboard Advertising

Blog Based Advertising

Business Development / Partnership Deals

Buying Your Competition / Mergers and Acquisition

Celebrity Endorsement

Cold Call Marketing

Door to Door Sales

Dream 100

Email Marketing

Facebook Advertising

Flyers

Google Maps

Google Reviews

Google Shopping

Magazine Advertising

Mall / Shopping Center Traffic

Mass Mailers

Mass Texting (Twilio)

Mass Voicemails (Slybroadcast)

Mass Emails (AWeber, Constant Contact)

Networking Intentionally (Set number of meetings per month and specific organizations)

Newspaper Advertising

Outdoor Signage

Pandora.com Radio Advertising

Pay Per Click - Search Engine Marketing / Advertising

Pop-Up Shop

Public Relations

Celebrity Tie-In Strategy
Expert Strategy
Giveback Strategy
National News Tie-In Strategy
Shock and Awe Strategy

Radio Advertising

Referral Based Advertising

Retargeting Online ads (See SEO Conversion checklist)

Search Engine Optimization (See next pages for details)

Sign-Based Marketing

Sign-Flipper Marketing

Social Media Advertising

Speech Based Marketing

Spotify Advertising

Targeted Online ads

Television Advertising

Text Marketing

Trade Show Advertising

Valpak Advertising

Yelp Reviews

YouTube Advertising

> **Bias Alert... But Still True**
>
> ThriveTime Show sponsors make more money than they spend on advertising.

Most buyers don't care at all about salespeople and especially YOU and I. Thus, you must learn that the world "I" has no real place in the world of sales. When you are first learning to really sell well, you are going to find yourself using the word "I" throughout your presentation in a way that is going to demotivate your potential buyer. However, overtime, with practice and intentionality you are going to quickly learn that you must think in terms of the buyer at all times.

CHAPTER 6
YOU MUST AVOID PUFFERY AT ALL COST

WHAT IS "PUFFERY?"

Puffery is simply anything that you cannot prove that you are verbally vomiting out of your mouth during a sales presentation. When selling, you want to maniacally obsess about avoiding saying unprovable statements like:

* We're Dallas' number one fitness bootcamp
  (unless you can prove it)

* We're the best automotive repair shop in our city
  (unless you can prove it)

* Save big money when you buy from us
  (unless you can show how much money you can actually save your ideal and likely buyers)

* We're the fastest service provider in our industry
  (unless you can prove it)

Buyers who have been on the planet for more than 15 years can usually smell and detect a B.S. sales claim from miles away and they no longer even take these sales claims seriously. As business owners and salespeople, it is vitally important that you recognize that the number one guaranteed and fastest way to kill a relationship and trust with your potential buyer is to claim that your business is "number one" without being able to support the claim that you are making.

However, when you are attempting to sell something to your ideal and likely buyers you must also understand that when you provide benefits (solutions) provided by facts (provable examples), potential buyers will respect you and actually take you seriously (the vast majority of the time). Here are a few examples of puffery in action:

* "As the best provider in our area it is incumbent on me to make sure that you don't waste your money with poor service providers."

* "Because we have been serving the Dallas area for over 20 years you can count on us for all of your custom home remodeling needs."

* "We are number one in our region."

CHAPTER 7

YOU MUST GET THE LAW OF CREDIBILITY TO WORK ON YOUR BEHALF

WHILE PLAYING THE GAME OF BUSINESS AND WHILE PLAYING THE GAME OF SALES IT IS VERY IMPORTANT FOR YOU TO UNDERSTAND THE LAW OF CREDIBILITY.

As a salesperson you must not ever say anything that you can't prove and you must be able to verifiably prove everything you say. When I was growing my first business www.DJConnection.com, I was obsessed with gathering feedback and reviews from each and every customer that I provided service for because I knew that they would be happy to recommend me to their family and friends because of the maniacal focus and preparation that I put into each and every event that I served as a disc jockey.

NOTABLE QUOTABLE

"Render more service than you are paid for and eventually you will be paid more for less services rendered."

– NAPOLEON HILL (THE BEST-SELLING SELF-HELP AUTHOR OF ALL-TIME AND THE PERSONAL APPRENTICE OF THE LATE GREAT ANDREW CARNEGIE)

I then used my references and reviews as a POWERFUL sales tool and you should too. In the game of sales it is vitally important you can provide proof of every claim that you are making to your ideal and likely buyers and it really does change the game when you are able to supply your potential buyers with verifiable references, video reviews and Google reviews that validate every claim that you make to your potential buyers.

HOW DO YOU GO ABOUT GATHERING REFERENCES AND REVIEWS FROM YOUR IDEAL AND LIKELY BUYERS?

Step 1 - You must "wow" each and every client as though they are the only client you are ever going to have. You must get your projects done early, under budget, and with a WOW that makes your ideal and likely buyers want to refer you now.

NOTABLE QUOTABLE

"Profit in business comes from repeat customers, customers that boast about your product and service, and that bring friends with them."

- W. Edwards Deming (The legendary American engineer, statistician, professor, author, lecturer, and management consultant who is celebrated for his work in Japan after WWII, particularly his work with the leaders of Japanese industry. That work began in July and August 1950, in Tokyo and at the Hakone Convention Center, when Deming delivered speeches on what he called "Statistical Product Quality Administration". Many in Japan credit Deming as one of the inspirations for what has become known as the Japanese post-war economic miracle of 1950 to 1960, when Japan rose from the ashes of war on the road to becoming the second-largest economy in the world through processes partially influenced by the ideas Deming taught.)

NOTABLE QUOTABLE

"If you make customers unhappy in the physical world, they might each tell 6 friends. If you make customers unhappy on the internet, they can each tell 6,000 friends."

- Jeff Bezos (The founder of Amazon.com)

NOTABLE QUOTABLE

"Whatever you do, do it well. Do it so well that when people see you do it, they will want to come back and see you do it again, and they will want to bring others and show them how well you do what you do."

- Walt Disney (The man who co-founded the Disney Empire, the original voice of Mickey Mouse and the man who forever changed the face of media.)

NOTABLE QUOTABLE

"We see our customers as invited guests to a party, and we are the hosts. It's our job every day to make every important aspect of the customer experience a little bit better."

- Jeff Bezos (The founder of Amazon.com who is now worth approximately $115.6 billion as of January 2020.)

Step 2 – Kindly and relentlessly follow-up with your former and current clients to gather reviews. Listed below I have included the actual script that our team uses on a weekly basis to gather reviews for a local cosmetic surgeon:

SCRIPT:

Hello is this the amazing _____?!

How are you today?

Hey, _____ this is _____ up here at Doctor _____'s office and this month he is having us survey former and current patients to see how happy you were with your overall experience...on a scale of 1 to 10 with 10 being the highest, how happy were you with the overall level of service that we provided?

And in your mind what could we improve the most?

IF A LOW SCORE – DON'T READ THE NEXT PART

Hey, we have a contest going until tonight, where any former patient who leaves us a review on Google before the end of the day will receive a $10 Starbucks gift card and is entered into a drawing to win a bunch of other discounts. Do you know how to leave a review?

First, just type in _____ Cosmetic Surgery and the word _____ (city). Second click on the reviews and just leave us a review there. Does that make sense?

Stay on the phone and coach them through getting a review...

What is your address that you want me to send the gift card to?

Step 3 - As you gather reviews, it is extremely important that you gather them in a way that is orderly, easily to present and verifiable. Don't remove the last names from your references and blur the faces of your former clients from their testimonial videos. In the world of sales, you are guilty until proven innocent in the eyes of the customer. Go out of your way to PROVE EVERYTHING THAT YOU ARE SAYING with great detail. At the beginning of each and every book I write, I go out of my way to supply potential readers and book buyers alike with a mountain of verifiable references from real clients that I have really coached to success over the years otherwise it won't seem like what I am saying is true. As an example, just this morning, Aaron Antis who is the marketing director of www.ShawHomes.com (which is the largest homebuilder in the state of Oklahoma and a long-time client) text me the following message:

> "Our January sales this year in comparison to last
> year are up 362%, just sold a few more. $9.8 million
> so far this month. Last year (in January) was $2.7
> million and we still have a week to go."

> - AARON ANTIS

ASSUME THAT THE POTENTIAL BUYER DOES NOT BELIEVE YOU

It is incumbent upon me to believe that you don't believe me and that I must hammer you with page after page of verifiable references. Why? Because we live in a world filled with shady sales people who will say and do anything to make a fast buck. Thus I invite you to call www.ShawHomes.com and to schedule a quick five-minute conversation with Aaron Antis to ask him whether in fact what I am writing here is true or not.

I was talking to one of my 5 ½ year clients, Steve Currington, who told me that his mortgage company had grown from a startup business to one that was now generating over $251 million dollars in annual mortgage sales per year since he's been working with me. Don't believe me? Text Steve Currington now at: (918) 281-5475.

In 2007 I was named as the United States Small Business Administration Entrepreneur of the Year for the State of Oklahoma. Don't believe me? Check out the image below:

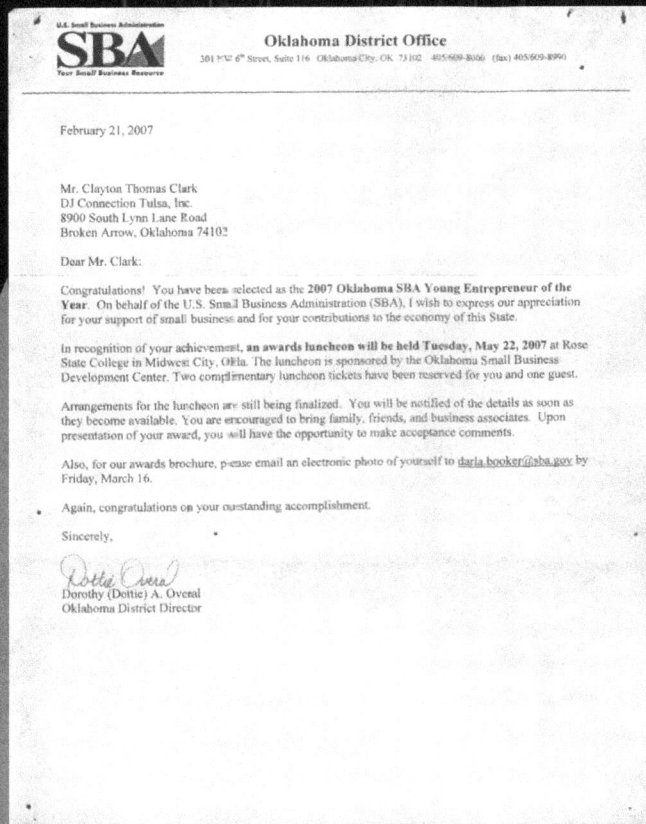

Oklahoma District Office
301 NW 6th Street, Suite 116 Oklahoma City, OK 73102   405/609-8000   (fax) 405/609-8990

February 21, 2007

Mr. Clayton Thomas Clark
DJ Connection Tulsa, Inc.
8900 South Lynn Lane Road
Broken Arrow, Oklahoma 74102

Dear Mr. Clark:

Congratulations! You have been selected as the **2007 Oklahoma SBA Young Entrepreneur of the Year**. On behalf of the U.S. Small Business Administration (SBA), I wish to express our appreciation for your support of small business and for your contributions to the economy of this State.

In recognition of your achievement, **an awards luncheon will be held Tuesday, May 22, 2007** at Rose State College in Midwest City, OKla. The luncheon is sponsored by the Oklahoma Small Business Development Center. Two complimentary luncheon tickets have been reserved for you and one guest.

Arrangements for the luncheon are still being finalized. You will be notified of the details as soon as they become available. You are encouraged to bring family, friends, and business associates. Upon presentation of your award, you will have the opportunity to make acceptance comments.

Also, for our awards brochure, please email an electronic photo of yourself to darla.booker@sba.gov by Friday, March 16.

Again, congratulations on your outstanding accomplishment.

Sincerely,

Dorothy (Dottie) A. Overal
Oklahoma District Director

Success is a choice. A choice to make trade-offs... a choice to get up early... a choice to skip lunch to hit a deadline... a choice to push through fear... a choice to work on the weekend to get ahead... a choice to turn off the TV and open a book... a choice to hold yourself and others accountable... success is a choice that I make every day.

CLAY CLARK
Founder of ThriveTimeShow.com, former U.S. SBA Entrepreneur of the Year, host of the ThriveTime Show, and America's #1 Business Coach

The average client that I coach increases their sales by 104% per year. Don't believe me? Check out:

https://www.thrivetimeshow.com/testimonials

Whether it is me, or it is you, who is trying to convince our ideal and likely buyers that we do know what we are talking about, it is SUPER IMPORTANT for you to recognize the power of gathering real and objective Google and video reviews / testimonials from real customers.

As you are gathering your references and reviews from your ideal and likely buyers keep in mind that your potential ideal and likely buyers love:

* Quantifiable results

* Compelling before and after photos

* References that your potential buyers can call and verify that what you are saying is in fact correct.

CHAPTER 8

THE POWER OF PROOF STATEMENTS

When buyers demonstrate a lack of trust or belief in what you are saying, it is also important for you to recognize that ALL POTENTIAL BUYERS are either aggressively or passive-aggressively demonstrating a lack of trust or belief in what you are saying at all times. Thus, you must never ever deliver a benefit (a solution that your company can provide) without also delivering a verifiable and provable fact with the statement. First, clearly state the benefit of what your product or service can offer and them immediately prove and support the benefit you just delivered using facts, statistics from third-party sources that are reputable (*Forbes*.com, FoxNews.com, CNN.com, Gallup.com, etc.).

HERE IS AN EXAMPLE OF THE PROOF STATEMENTS THAT WE USE WHEN SELLING ON BEHALF OF THE TULSA COSMETIC SURGEON, DOCTOR BRYAN WHITLOCK:

BENEFITS:

* 1st - Dr. Bryan is currently the highest rated and most reviewed cosmetic surgeon in Tulsa because the man is obsessed with making sure that every patient is super happy with every aspect of their interaction with us from the consultation, to the actual procedures to the followup after the procedure.

* 2nd - Dr. Whitlock personally meets with every potential patient before each and every procedure to make sure that you have all of your questions answered and to make sure that he can tell you exactly what the procedure is going to cost right down to the penny so that you won't have any surprise expenses.

* 3rd - Dr. Whitlock prides himself on being the most affordable cosmetic surgery center in Tulsa, so he has no money down and 100% financing options that he can talk to you about so that everybody can afford to get the procedures done that they feel they need.

PROOF STATEMENTS HELP YOUR CAUSE / NOT USING A PROOF STATEMENT HURTS YOUR CAUSE

Even if your ideal and likely buyer does not express concern about you not having a proof statement to support the statement / benefit that you just spoke of, e-mailed or delivered in some way, you must remember that your potential buyer does not trust you unless you support every claim you make with facts. In the world of sales, you are guilty until proven innocent and YOU MUST OBSESS ABOUT DELIVERING FACTS to support each and every claim / statement / benefit that you make.

When you get in the habit of always delivering proof to support every claim that you ever make, you will discover that this wows customers and allows them to feel more comfortable with you and your team. Your potential buyers will appreciate the fact that you actually took the time to prepare for them and they will admire the confidence and competence that this creates. When you are selling at this level you are in a whole different league than 95% of other salespeople who simply make up statistics on the fly, who make bogus claims, who exaggerate product benefits and who are simply poorly prepared and perpetually dishonest at best.

WHY DON'T ALL SALESPEOPLE INVEST THE TIME NEEDED TO GATHER FACTS TO SUPPORT THE BENEFITS, CLAIMS, PRODUCTS AND SERVICES THEY ARE PROMOTING?

Most people are lazy most of the time and even when presented with the facts most people refuse to act. Most people seek wisdom, but only act to avoid pain. You must become a proactive and prepared sales professional if you want to win in the world of business and sales.

FUN FACTS:

"78 percent of the men interviewed had cheated on their current partner." – 5 Myths About Cheating

https://www.washingtonpost.com/opinions/five-myths-about-cheating/2012/02/08/gIQANGdaBR_story.html?noredirect=on&utm_term=.05ab54a87466

"75% of employees steal from the workplace and most do so repeatedly."

https://www.cbsnews.com/news/employee-theft-are-you-blind-to-it/

"85% of job applicants lie on resumes."

https://www.inc.com/jt-odonnell/staggering-85-of-job-applicants-lying-on-resumes-.html

CHAPTER 9

CONSTRUCTING THE ULTIMATE SCALABLE SALES SYSTEM

IN ORDER FOR YOU TO BUILD THE ULTIMATE SCALABLE SALES SYSTEM YOU ARE GOING TO HAVE CREATE OR GATHER THE FOLLOWING SALES TOOLS (AND DON'T TELL ME YOU DON'T HAVE TIME):

NOTABLE QUOTABLE

"Ninety-nine percent of the failures come from people who have the habit of making excuses."

GEORGE WASHINGTON CARVER

(A man who was born a slave, yet went on to become America's leading agricultural scientist. George Washington Carver recognized that the newly freed slaves were aggressively depleting their soil of nutrients by perpetually planting only cotton, thus he was determined to solve the problem. George Washington Carver knew that planting sweet potatoes and peanuts into the soil would restore minerals and nutrients to the soil, but he knew that there really wasn't a huge market for sweet potatoes or peanuts. So what did he do? He obsessively focused on developing financially viable products that could be made using sweet potatoes and peanuts. It was George Washington Carver who was responsible for returning fertility to the soil and allowing his newly freed people to become financially

When I was building my first business (www.DJConnection.com) I worked at three jobs in order to afford the Yellow Page advertising and the equipment needed to get the company off of the ground. While working at Applebee's, Target and DirecTV I found myself stretched thin; but I made it happen and YOU CAN TOO. You must block out time to create these sales documents.

NOTABLE QUOTABLE

"You either pay now or pay later with just about every decision you make about where and how you spend your time."

Lee Cockerell
(Time Management Magic: How To Get More Done Every Day And Move From Surviving To Thriving)

Today, I wake up at 3:00 AM each morning and I go to bed at 9 PM in order to find the time needed to turn my dreams into reality and in order run the various businesses I am involved with.

NOTABLE QUOTABLE

"A Carnegie or a Rockefeller or a James J. Hill or a Marshall Field accumulates a fortune through the applications of the same principles available to all of us, but we envy them and their wealth without ever thinking of studying their philosophy and applying it to ourselves. We look at a successful person in the hour of their triumph and wonder how they did it, but we overlook the importance of analyzing their methods. And we forget the price they had to pay in the careful, well-organized preparation that had to be made before they could reap the fruits of their efforts."

- NAPOLEON HILL
(The best-selling self-help author of all-time)

In order for you to become super successful in the world of sales, you are going to have to learn to say no to some things. What do you have to say no to in order to find the time needed to create the life changing documents and sales tools listed above?

_____

_____

_____

_____

_____

_____

_____

_____

_____

"Until you value yourself, you will not value your time.
Until you value your time, you will not do anything with it.

Lee Cockerell
(Time Management Magic: How To Get More Done Every Day And
Move From Surviving To Thriving)

CHAPTER 10
DIAGRAM YOUR SALES PLAN

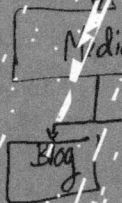

NOTABLE QUOTABLE

"Where there is no revelation, people cast off restraint; but blessed is the one who heeds wisdom's instruction."

- PROVERBS 29:18
(THE NEW INTERNATIONAL VERSION OF THE BIBLE)

Very few people on the planet can form a clear mental picture of something as abstract and esoteric as a sales script and a scalable sales system unless you can provide them with a diagram of how the entire sales process should look moving from left to right. In the world of business, diagrams like this are known as a workflow. Pictured is the workflow that I have created to map out what a scalable sales system should look like. But before we get into the diagram, what does it mean to be scalable? In order for you to ever create a business model / system that has power to create both time and financial freedom, you must learn how to create systems that are repeatable, doable, and executable by people who are not you. If you create a system that only you can replicate, you will lose your time freedom as you are gaining your financial freedom. As you build your business systems and plans, focus on making sure that they are implementable by "normal people (like me)" and not only by geniuses like you. Don't create a system that only you can understand, or you, my friend, are creating an unscalable business model.

NOTABLE QUOTABLE

"I try to invest in businesses that are so wonderful that an idiot can run them. Because sooner or later, one will."

- Warren Buffett
(The billionaire investor who started with nothing, but who is now worth $87.3 billion according to *Forbes*)

DAILY SALES KEY PERFORMANCE INDICATORS

1. How many outbound calls were made?

2. How many appointments were made?

3. How many deals were closed?

4. Why did people say no?

Base Sales KPI's on the super star sales person, not the average in the group.

Keep team accountable to KPI's with short, daily standing meetings.

> "You don't have to be a doctor to build a sales focused culture. However, you do need a PHD: Pig-Headed Discipline."

CLAY CLARK
Co-Host of the ThriveTime Business Coach Radio Show and member of the Forbes Coaches Council

Step 1 A Lead Comes Into Your Business (Via Email, Voicemail, Text, Etc.)	Step 2 Send the ideal and likely buyer a text / email that communicates the following - Thank you for reaching out to us. We will get in touch with you as soon as humanly possible. We strive to provide great service, but don't take our word for it. Click on the link below to view recent testimonials from real clients just like you.	Step 3 - Call, text and email the ideal and likely buyer until they cry, buy or die. (FUN FACT: We have to reach out to the average ThrivtimeShow.com conference attendee 20 + times before we reach them on average. Why? People don't answer the phone unless they recognize the number. The average entrepreneur is super busy. God is trying to teach us something.)	Step 4 - When calling your ideal and likely buyer implement the proven sales system: 1. Rapport 2. Needs 3. Benefits 4. Call to Action 5. Isolate Objections 6. Call to Action Again	Step 5 - Email the potential client a confirmation of the time at which you will be meeting and additional references.
Create 1 Box to Demonstrate This	Create 1 Box to Demonstrate This	Create 1 Box to Demonstrate This	Create 6 Boxes to Demonstrate This	Create 1 Box to Demonstrate This

When building a sales script you must keep in mind that the sales script that you are creating must be scalable, learnable and repeatable by the actual humans that work with you and who are not you. Don't make your script complicated and hard to learn or your sales team will never be able to scale and you must provide your salespeople with a NO-BRAINER SALES OFFER that is so good that your ideal and likely buyers simply cannot reject it as an example:

* www.DrBreck.com – Dr. Breck has chosen to offer a free exam, a free x-ray and a free adjustment to any first-time patient who chooses to schedule a first visit with his chiropractic practice.

* www.DRZoellner.com – When you visit Dr. Zoellner's office you can get 1 pair of stylish eyeglasses and an eye exam for only $99.

* www.EITRLounge.com – Your first haircut at Elephant In The Room is just $1 and we actually donate that dollar to www.Compassion.com.

* www.MakeYourLifeEpic.com / www.ThrivetimeShow.com – Although I run the nation's most successful one-on-one business coaching program, I do not charge a dime for your initial consultation with me so that you and I can connect to find out whether we would be a good fit to work together. This first appointment and consultation normally takes 1 hour of my time, and is actually something that I really do look forward to doing each and every time.

* www.ShawHomes.com – At the time I am writing this book, ShawHomes.com is offering a free Master Bath Shower Upgrade plus they will pay your closing costs until January 31st.

I am going to briefly walk you through the various portions of the sales script that you are going to have to write and then I am going to provide you with an ample example that the average human mind can handle.

OVERALL YOU MUST SCRIPT OUT THE FOLLOWING ASPECTS OF YOUR SALES SYSTEM (SCRIPTS):

* Rapport
* Needs
* Benefits

* Call to Action
* Isolate Objections
* Recall to Action

RAPPORT:

When scripting out the rapport portion of your sales script you must keep the following pieces of information in your mind.

1. The goal is to get the potential buyer to both like and trust you.

2. The potential buyer (the prospect you are talking to) must talk 70% of the time.

3. When writing your script make sure to avoid asking questions that can be answered in one word and questions that attack the buyer. Don't ask questions that are patronizing. As an example, approximately 6 months ago, I went onto the car lot of a dealership and the salesperson asked me, "Now are we looking to buy today or are we just looking to look around?"

4. You want to ask the buyer questions that require them to strongly think about the answer and to have to search for the answer they provide; such as:

   * "So tell me...what research have you done so far about the other business coaching companies in our industry?"

   * "What is the main thing that you are really looking to get out of your business coaching experience and what are you not wanting to get out of your business coaching experience?"

5. You must script out a maximum of 5 minutes or approximately five rapport building questions for this portion of the script.

NEEDS:

When scripting out the needs portion of your sales script. you must keep the following things in mind:

1. The goal is to find the problems that your ideal and likely buyer has that you can actually solve.

2. The potential buyer must believe that you understand where they are versus where they want to be.

3. Your script must allow the potential buyer to talk. Your script must allow your ideal and likely buyer to share and to explain their needs with great detail as opposed to the sales presentations of most salespeople that involve the salesperson verbally vomiting on their potential buyers for 30 minutes. Most sales people don't know what they should be doing so they typically just spend time serving up a verbal buffet filled with industry jargon, features that no-one cares about, and patronizing questions that potential buyers can answer with one word.

4. The questions that you are scripting out during this portion of your sales script should cause your potential ideal and likely buyers to deliver well thought out answers. When you produce a script that results in your ideal and likely buyers providing fast answers you know that your script is not good.

5. If possible (based upon your industry), you want to script out questions that will cause your ideal and likely buyers to dream big and to think about the how their world could in fact be just a little bit better such as:

* In a perfect world, what is the main thing that you are looking to get out of your wedding photography experience?

* So in your mind, what is the main thing that you are looking to get out of your next men's grooming and haircut experience?

* Assuming that all graphic design companies charged the same price, what is truly the main thing that you are looking to get out of the next graphic design firm that you hire?

6. You must script out a maximum of five minutes or approximately five needs-based questions for this portion of the script.

7. Make sure that the scripts you write can be read and communicated by somebody who is not you.

NOTABLE QUOTABLE

"I try to invest in businesses that are so wonderful that an idiot can run them. Because sooner or later, one will."

- WARREN BUFFETT
(THE BILLIONAIRE INVESTOR WHO STARTED WITH NOTHING, BUT WHO IS NOW WORTH $87.3 BILLION ACCORDING TO *FORBES*)

BENEFITS:

When writing out and scripting the benefits portion of your script you must remember that the goal of this portion of the script is to demonstrate clearly to your potential ideal and likely buyer what problems that your business can solve for them in a provable and verifiable way.

1. When scripting out the benefits portion of your script limit yourself to five minutes and approximately five benefits for the benefits portion of the script.

2. Make sure that the benefits you are describing actually solve the problems of your ideal and likely buyers.

3. When writing the benefits portion of your sales scripts assume that the person listening to you reading your sales scripts does not believe you. When possible provide provable statistics, testimonials and references.

4. Make sure that the scripts you write can be read, and communicated by somebody who is not you.

CALL TO ACTION:

When writing out the call to action portion of your sales script you must realize that most people by default are adverse to taking action. Thus, you as a salesperson must call the person to take action one step at a time.

1. When scripting out the call to action portion of the script make sure to that you include at least five questions that will eventually lead to you setting a specific time to meet with your ideal and likely buyer to see if the products or services that you provide are a good fit.

2. Make sure that your script is actually executable by the kind of people who are able to afford to employ.

3. Make sure that the scripts you write can be read, and communicated by somebody who is not you.

NOTABLE QUOTABLE

"I try to invest in businesses that are so wonderful that an idiot can run them. Because sooner or later, one will."

- WARREN BUFFETT
(THE BILLIONAIRE INVESTOR WHO STARTED WITH NOTHING, BUT WHO IS NOW WORTH $87.3 BILLION ACCORDING TO FORBES)

ISOLATE OBJECTIONS:

When writing this portion of your call script you must recognize that the vast majority of sales are closed after the consumer has posed at least one or two objections. You must understand that people with a sound mind are going to always have concerns, questions and objections that they will pose before just blindly handing over their hard-earned money to a salesperson whom they just met. Write a script that teaches your salespeople to expect rejections and how to deal with them in a way that is educational, kind and not patronizing. When you take the time to script out and to deliver questions about each and every objection that you receive, you will find that nearly half of the objections go away simply by you clarifying what the objection is.

1. When scripting out the isolate objections portion of the call script you want to make sure that your team can replicate what you are teaching. Fight the resistance to write out principles and mindsets instead of the actual text that you want your team to read each and every time.

2. When your sales team gets in trouble, their overwhelming natural response by default is to start fast-talking and to start saying things that will not help their cause. Thus, you must invest the time needed to script out the things that you want your team to say whenever your salesperson:

* Loses their place in a sales presentation

* Forgets what to do next

* Gets attacked by your potential ideal and likely buyer

* Gets stuck in a situation where the overall sales pitch is moving at a rapid rate and they need to buy extra time to regain their focus and to gather their thoughts

3. I highly recommend downloading and printing off the document that I have created call the "Deal Wheel" and placing it in the cubicles of your sales team of somewhere prominent where they will be able to use it during their times of need:

Empathize

A. The Move: Repeat back what the potential buyer just said in the form of a question.
B. Allow the buyer to know that you are listening actively.
C. EXAMPLE: *"So what you are saying is that _____."*

Appreciate

A. The Move: This move is often referred to as the "Wounded Dog."
B. Suck air in through your teeth and sound as though you accidentally stepped on your baby puppy when speaking.
C. EXAMPLE: *"I can appreciate that. Let me ask you, what do you mean by that?"*

THE DEAL WHEEL

This move is designed to avoid any direct conflict with the objection.

1
2
4
3

Supporting Benefit

A. The Move: This move draws its power from the Law of Credibility.
B. Support every claim you make with fact.
C. EXAMPLE: *"You know, you are exactly right in fact. In fact many of our clients originally felt the same way you now do when we first started working with them. And what they found is that _____ (benefit supported by a fact). So let me ask you _____ (go right back into where you were in your presentation before the objection was first presented by the potential buyer)."*

Ask Leading Question

A. The Move: This move is designed avoid any direct conflict with the objection.
B. Sound as though you are sincerely asking the question because you should be sincerely asking the question.
C. EXAMPLE: *"Assuming that _____ was not an issue. In your mind what is the main reason that you are looking to _____ (buy a house, buy insurance, promote your company, hire an accountant, the action item they are looking to do)."*

4. At this point it almost goes without saying, but it is imperative that you make sure that the script you are writing is actually executable by the type of humans that you are able to afford to hire within your organization.

5. Make sure that the scripts you write can be read, and communicated by somebody who is not you.

NOTABLE QUOTABLE

"I try to invest in businesses that are so wonderful that an idiot can run them. Because sooner or later, one will."

- WARREN BUFFETT
(THE BILLIONAIRE INVESTOR WHO STARTED WITH NOTHING, BUT WHO IS NOW WORTH $87.3 BILLION ACCORDING TO *FORBES*)

To help make the process of creating a call script less overwhelming I have included the actual call script that I created for a company that they used in route to becoming a multi-million dollar company:

RAPPORT:

"Hello and thank you for calling _____ Videography this is
_____, how may I help you?

What date have you all decided upon?

What's your fiance's name?

Where will your event be held at? (Compliment location with
CONVICTION)

What made you choose that venue?

NEEDS:

So are you wanting to have us take most of the video shots
indoors or outdoors?

So what time do you all anticipate starting that actual ceremony
and the wedding day festivities?

In terms of personality, are you looking for a really fun-loving
videographer or one that is more laid back? If a 1 is a fly on the

wall and a 10 is very interactive, how interactive of a videographer are you looking for on a scale of 1 to 10?

Do you guys like more of the classic traditional style, which is more posed out or the photo journalistic style with more of the candid shots? (most brides do a mix)

How many guests are you all expecting? (So you are kind of a big deal?)

BENEFITS:

How many videographers are you wanting?

How familiar are you overall with _____ videography?

At _____ videography there are basically five things that we do that no other videography company in our area is doing:

Benefit 1: We are the only videography company that lets you choose the style of videography you want. With our unique system, our event planners invest time with every client before they decide to book with us, to go over the videography styles that are most popular today. Otherwise it would be kind of like letting someone else choose your wedding gown for you.

Benefit 2: We include a comprehensive timeline planning service. (pause) Over the years we've found that the best way to capture your candid moments is to know where you are going to be and when you'll be there, so we include this service with every package. We'll do the homework ahead of time so that on the day of your wedding you can relax and know that we are all on the same page.

Benefit 3: We are the only company out there offering UNLIMITED TIME with each and every package. (pause) You're going to spend months planning the wedding, so we're not going to make you feel rushed and pressured to cram your entire wedding day into a 4 hour window of time. With our unlimited time packages we will arrive at your ceremony 3 hours before it starts and we'll be out there all night just in case someone's grandma is breaking it down on the dance floor at 2:00 am.

videos is now 3-5 months, which is why we are so excited to offer a 2 week turn-around time. Because of the systems that we have in place our editors are now able to get your video back to you in 2 weeks instead of 6 months.

CALL TO ACTION:

Now terms of price, because we do so many weddings and corporate events, our prices tend to be about 30% less than any other award-winning videographers in the industry...And based upon what we've talked about, I would definitely recommend that you would consider the _____ or the _____ packages and those packages are normally _____ or _____ (PAUSE). However, with the _____ special, which is good until this weekend, you'd actually be looking at _____ or _____. Basically, the only difference between the packages is _____ And as far as securing your date, we require a 25% non-refundable retainer for each package and that goes towards the package price. The remaining balance is not actually due until 1 week before the date of your event, so you guys have plenty of time to take care of it.

Now I know you all stay busy planning the wedding, but with your schedule do you and your fiance both work mostly during the day or at night?

So who all is helping you to plan out your big day? What most brides like to do is to set up a time where we talk with you and your fiance. That way you all can interrogate us as a team and even make our event planner cry if needed.

Well just looking here at the day timer...our schedule is just so packed with the Bridal Fairs we have just done...but how would _____ or _____ work? (example: Tuesday 5:30 or 6:00 pm) work for you or maybe even a weekend?

Great...and what phone number should I list with your file? Is there an E-MAIL Address that I could EMAIL you all directions at? And I'm going to email you some references from some recent weddings we've done, and a brief company history overview so you can do your research. That way you can call some actual previous customers to interrogate them. Now are you familiar with where we are located? Basically, we are located _____.

Benefit 4: We have proactive videographers that are comfortable leading the way. (pause) Most brides tell us that they are concerned that their videographer will be very pushy or kind of an artistic diva while other brides tell us that they are worried that their videographer won't direct them enough. We just want to find out where you fall in that range.

Now in terms of the videographers themselves, we know most companies have just one or two videographers, but we focus on more of a team element because we don't want the overall health of your wedding to be dependent upon the health of just one videographer. And professionally speaking....We will not send out a videographer dressed like a ninja (Ha, ha). All of our videographers will be dressed professionally.

Benefit 5: We are the only videography company offering a 2-WEEK TURN-AROUND TIME for every wedding that we shoot. (pause) According to Modern Bride & theKnot.com, they say that the average turn-around-time for wedding

CHAPTER 11

THE ART OF THE COLD CALL + LEARNING TO LOVE REJECTION

For most people on the planet, when they are told that they need to make cold calls they feel as though they have been condemned to experience the hell of earth known as rejection. However, when I was first starting DJConnection.com, I quickly came to the conclusion that nobody on the planet was waking up with a burning desire to reach out to me to find out what services and products that I offered and to pay me. Thus, I quickly came to the conclusion that if it was going to be it was up to me. And thus cold-calling was going to be something that I had to do and that I had to master as soon as possible. Luckily for me, previous to starting DJConnection.com full-time I had worked full-time as a cold caller for DirecTV, West Telecommunications and Faith Highway. However, in order to teach you the art of the cold call, I am going to work off of the assumption that you have never made outbound calls and that you are going to need to be taught the rules of the game. But, before I teach you these rules, please understand that entire successful companies have been built using the power of the cold-calls scripts that I have written and helped my clients to implement.

THESE INCLUDE:

www.500KMSP.com

www.ClayStaires.com

www.DJConnection.com

www.EpicPhotos.com

www.FearsClark.com

www.FullPackageMedia.com

www.RedmondGrowth.com

Hear their stories at
www.thrivetimeshow.com/testimonials.

SO WITHOUT ANY FURTHER ADO, HERE ARE THE 6 COLD-CALLING RULES OF THE GAME:

* Rule #1 - Most of your ideal and likely buyers will have a decent life and a decent day if they never meet you.

* Rule #2 - Most of your ideal and likely buyers feel as though their life is good enough without buying your product or service.

* Rule #3 - Most of your ideal and likely buyers do not want to change what they are doing now, because they believe that it will be too much trouble to change.

* Rule #4 - None of the people that you are calling are going to be super excited to hear about the new and improved features of the products and services that you are attempting to sell.

* Rule #5 - Unless you are able to quickly find the areas of dissatisfaction in the lives of the ideal and likely buyers that you are calling you will not ever schedule an appointment, close a deal, or sell something.

* Rule #6 - Until you have created a call script that can quickly and scalably find the areas of dissatisfaction in the lives of the ideal and likely buyers that you are calling you will not ever be ever to each a team of people to schedule an appointment, close a deal, or sell something.

FEUER

NOTRUF

I realize that what I just wrote might sound like the dream-killing demotivational message that you did not need in your life right now, but now without any further ado I am going to share with you 9 basic cold-calling rules that help you to succeed:

* Cold-Calling Rule #1 - Stick to the script. Most people who attempt to cold-call for a living immediately deviate from the script the first time that they encounter a question from their ideal and likely buyer or any type of adversity and this is a recipe for disaster. When in doubt, stick to the script.

* Cold-Calling Rule #2 - Dial and smile. When you are on the phone with your ideal and likely buyers it is CRITICAL that you smile while you dial. Your potential ideal and likely buyer can hear whether you are smiling or not because they have a brain that works (most of the time).

* Cold-Calling Rule #3 - The pros go slow and only an ass goes fast. I realize that sounds harsh, but it is true. Today's buyers quickly pickup when they are talking to a fast-talking huckster. Be intentional about talking slow and succinctly. Make sure that you inneculate each and every word that you speak in a clear and intentional manner.

* Cold-Calling Rule #4 - Don't use big words or industry jargon when cold-calling. Whenever you and I work too hard to sound too smart we get rejected by our ideal and likely buyers as a reward.

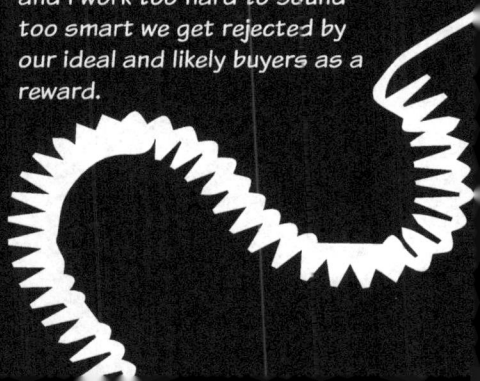

NOTABLE QUOTABLE

"If you can't explain it simply, you don't understand it well enough."

Albert Einstein

* Cold-Calling Rule #5 - Block out time to get into the mindset needed to grind. When you start cold-calling you must get yourself into the proper mindset and that requires time. When people play basketball, golf or tennis typically they warm-up before competing and going all out. The same is true when cold-calling. You must block out specific times in your schedule for dialing and smiling.

* Cold-Calling Rule #6 - Don't sound like you've consumed 14 energy drinks before calling your ideal and likely buyer. You want to sound enthusiastic, but you also want to make sure that at all times you sound professional. It is imperative that at all times you sound in control, credible and not crazy (but, not too dull).

* Cold-Calling Rule #7 - Assume the close at all times when cold-calling. When you are cold-calling people that you don't know you must mentally commit to the belief that everybody is fired up about what you are selling and this must come across in your voice.

* Cold-Calling Rule #8 - Record your calls and determine where your obvious fails are. When you are cold-calling it is incredibly important that you listen to your calls on an on-going basis so that you will know that you are doing wrong and how you can improve.

* Cold-Calling Rule #9 - If your name is difficult to leave with a secretary or the gate-keeper change the name you leave to something that is easier to understand, grasp and write down.

IT IS POSSIBLE TO SUCCESSFULLY COLD CALL IN THE YEAR 2021

To build your faith that it is actually possible to build a successful business via cold-calling in the year 2021 I have attached the actual script that we use to make cold calls on behalf of one of our clients.

Rapport (On the Phone with the Front Desk Person)

*   Hey! I am looking for an IT consultant or MSP is that what you guys do?

*   I was wanting to know if *name on call list* is available; I am looking at his LinkedIn profile and wanted to speak with him/her.

*   Yes, you're speaking to him.

*   Great, how are you doing?

*   I'm good, and you?

*   I'm great! I am thinking of stopping after work and picking up a ferret! (HAHAHA)

*   Whatever they say...

*   Well _____(Name) the reason for my call is because I work for a company called _____ and according to your LinkedIn profile you look like a lot of the companies we work with. I'm calling on behalf of my boss, Mr. _____, who grows MSP companies to create time freedom for people like you.

*   Are you familiar with _____ (name of company)?

*   No.

*   We work with MSPs with around 5-10 people (whatever list we are going off of for the number of employees) to help them

grow their business. We have no clue if we could help you out or not, but my boss _____ wanted me to reach out to you to set up a quick 5 minute phone call to see if we could both benefit from a business relationship. Most people we speak with find out that a simple 5 minute phone call can completely change the course of their business, and so I was wanting to know _____(Name) if a five minute call sometime next week would be something worth your time to you?

What do you guys do?

* I know you're in the IT world so this might be a dumb question, but are you in front of a computer?

* Well, his site is _____ and he wanted to set up a 5 minute call... with you so that you could... hear about business growth systems directly from him, and decide whether we are a good fit to hang up on or to help you grow your business. Does that make sense?

* I know that sounds a bit generic, so The BEST way to see how we can help you would be to set up a quick 5 minute call with one of our Founders, _____

* And I have their calendar pulled up right, now would Tuesday or Thursday work better for you?

Close:

* Now for that 5 minute call, I'm showing that the first availability is on _____ or _____...which time works best for you?

* What is the best number for Mr _____ to reach you at?

* I'm going to send you a quick recap with Three POWERFUL things in it:

* 1st - Testimonials from real clients

* 2nd - Mr. _____'s biography and history

* 3rd - A 2-minute How it Works video

What email address should I send that to?

* Just to confirm, I have you down for _____ day at _____ time. Do you have it in your calendar?

* (Repeat the email spelling back to them)

* And if you could take 2 minutes to look at the link that I am sending you...IN FACT...I'm going to go ahead and text it to you as soon as we get off the phone...what number do you want for me to text the link to?

* I know that it will answer the questions that most people have which is who in the heck is this guy and should I take the phone call with _____.

* And to make it a good use of your time, Mr. _____would like

to show examples of every system that they are referencing so that you can verify that they weren't born yesterday and that they are not making stuff up. Do you think you can be in front of a computer for the meeting? Or right hand man or woah-man (woman) HAHA... By the way, how many employees do you guys have?

* (Bring the conviction layer) And I promise you this will not be a waste of time, so you can look forward to this in your calendar. Great, well I know that he looks forward to speaking with you on _____ (date) and _____ (time).

* (Add number of employees to appointment notes)

OBJECTION - Can I take a message / can you send me an email?

* Absolutely, are you in front of computer?

* Jump on our website, https://500kmsp.com/ so you can see his systems in action, again that's https://500kmsp.com/.

* His system is unlike any other in the industry, and it's really focused on creating both financial and time freedom for the owner.

* Basically _____ and _____ will actually teach you their proven system and strategies while helping you to execute the plan, for less than $2,000 per month. So he wanted to talk to you for 5 minutes to see if you are a good fit. And if you hate

his guts just hang up on him.

* So are mornings or afternoons better for you?

FAQS / COMMON OBJECTIONS:

What do you do? / What Type of IT Service?

* Well, our founder asked me personally to call you today because he has built and sold multiple million dollar plus MSPs and he believes that he can help your MSP in the same way.

What is this program overall?

* We help IT companies grow, we help with all of the things that a small business needs to free you up to run your company. We then coach you one on one in the proven strategies that have allowed the founders to be successful.

What is your website address?

* www.500KMSP.com, our marketing team and a ton of our references can also be found at 500KMSP.com.

No Time

* That is exactly why _____ and _____ built this program, they too struggled early on with juggling all of the things necessary to run a small business, and they now offer those proven strategies to small business owners like yourself.

We Already Have Our Own In-House Marketing Team \ We Already Use a Coach

* Awesome, do you mind me asking who you are working with and what your impression has been with their program?

* Do they help with lead generation, marketing, sales and closing strategies?

* Do they offer contract templates, and pre-written business documents?

* Do they offer one-on-one coaching?

* Our program offers all of these and much more, check out our website www.500kmsp.com for more information.

No Money

* (Suck air through the teeth)...so what's your main concern?

* I can appreciate that...what do you mean by that?

* I know we have packages for any budget, let me ask you, if _____was not an issue, what do you see as being the main benefit of being able to make your marketing all turn-key?

* You know you are exactly right.

* In fact most of the companies that we now work with originally felt the same way you do..and they found themselves in a little bit of a cash flow crisis...

* And what they found was that with the _____ MSP Coaching program, they are now able to close more deals and free up that cash.

* And it's a win-win because they now have a true partner in a MSP Coach.

* Basically we don't make money unless you make money.

* Does that make sense?

* Back into the script.

No Need

* (Suck air through the teeth)...so what's your main concern?

* I can appreciate that...what do you mean by that?

* You're right and we are hearing this from most MSP owners that we talk to and what's great is that Mr. _____ system

will actually help you keep more of the money that you bring in and close more deals.

* So...basically when you talk to Mr. _____ for 5 minutes you'll see how he can help you generate over $200,000 in revenue per employee, or you can hang up on him...

* Does that make sense?

* Back into the script.

How did you get my information?

* Although we only work with One Local MSP provider in each city, my boss provided me with a list of most of the local MSP companies in your area to call so that we can find out who is the best fit.

* Does that make sense?

Pricing - How much is it?

* (Suck air through the teeth)...I want Mr. _____ to be able to go over all of the details with you, but I know that we have packages for all budgets, but our total turn-key packages start as low as $1,000 per month and I have never seen us be unable to work with a business owner because of budgetary concerns.

* I have more business than I can handle.

* Suck air through your teeth? Let me ask you, what exactly do you mean by that?

* Well you know you are exactly right, in fact most of the clients that we work with today originally said the same thing when we first talked to them, and what they found is that our system will allow you to free up your schedule and increase your profitability...and that's why I would like to setup a 5 minute phone call with the founder, _____ and if we are not a good fit you can hang up on us.

* Now with your schedule, when are you most free...10 AM or sometime in the afternoon?

How long have you been doing this?

* _____ and the team have actually been doing this since October 15th of 1996 when ____ and _____ started their first IT company. They now help coach other MSP owners helping them become as successful as they are..

Any Question?

* You know that's a great question and that's why I would love to have Mr. _____ talk to you because we work with people with the same situation all of the time.

LEARNING TO VIEW REJECTION AS JUST ANOTHER STEP IN THE RIGHT DIRECTION

If you are going to become successful in the world of sales you must learn to love rejection and to view it as a prerequisite to your ultimate success. You must learn to view each rejection as just another step in the right direction. You must train your mind to understand that strength is only gained through struggle and that each "NO" that you receive is ultimately getting one step closer to the ultimate achievement of the goals you are pursuing. Once you learn how to train your mind to no longer emotionally process rejection as a bad thing you are nearly unstoppable.

When I think about persistence, I often think about Og Mandino and his book The Greatest Salesman in the World. During one portion of the book he wrote,

"I WILL PERSIST UNTIL I SUCCEED. THE PRIZES OF LIFE ARE AT THE END OF EACH JOURNEY, NOT NEAR THE BEGINNING; AND IT IS NOT GIVEN TO ME TO KNOW HOW MANY STEPS ARE NECESSARY IN ORDER TO REACH MY GOAL...ALWAYS WILL I TAKE ANOTHER STEP. IF THAT IS OF NO AVAIL I WILL TAKE ANOTHER, AND YET ANOTHER. IN TRUTH, ONE STEP AT A TIME IS NOT TOO DIFFICULT.

I WILL PERSIST UNTIL I SUCCEED.

HENCEFORTH, I WILL CONSIDER EACH DAY'S EFFORT AS BUT ONE BLOW OF MY BLADE AGAINST A MIGHTY OAK. THE FIRST BLOW MAY CAUSE NOT A TREMOR IN THE WOOD, NOR THE SECOND, NOR THE THIRD. EACH BLOW, OF ITSELF, MAY BE TRIFLING, AND SEEM OF NO CONSEQUENCE. YET FROM CHILDISH SWIPES THE OAK WILL EVENTUALLY TUMBLE. SO IT WILL BE WITH MY EFFORTS TODAY.

I WILL BE LIKEN TO THE RAIN DROP WHICH WASHES AWAY THE MOUNTAIN; THE ANT WHO DEVOURS A TIGER; THE STAR WHICH BRIGHTENS THE EARTH...I WILL BUILD MY CASTLE ONE BRICK AT A TIME FOR I KNOW THAT SMALL ATTEMPTS, REPEATED, WILL COMPLETE ANY UNDERTAKING.

I WILL PERSIST UNTIL I SUCCEED."

Og Mandino

THE GREATEST SALESMAN IN THE WORLD

CHAPTER 12

EVEN WITH GREAT SALES SYSTEMS, WITHOUT K.P.I.'S (KEY PERFORMANCE INDICATORS) YOUR SALES WILL DIE

IN ORDER FOR YOUR COMPANY TO SUCCEED YOU MUST HAVE A TEAM OF PEOPLE WHO ARE DIALING AND SMILING UNTIL THEIR FINGERS BLEED!

(FROM DIALING ALL THE NUMBERS)

It doesn't matter how skilled your team is and how much training they have received if they are simply not on the phone dialing and smiling. So you must determine right here and how the following outcomes that you will demand your team to deliver on a daily basis:

How many outbound calls do you require each of your sales representatives to make on a weekly basis? _____

_____

How many appointments do you want each of your sales representatives to schedule on a weekly basis? _____

_____

How many deals do you want each of your sales representatives to close on a weekly basis? _____

_____

AMPLE EXAMPLE

Go to Youtube and search "Call Center Management | The Art of Creating Luck | Tulsa PR Firm" to see an ample example that human mind can handle of what a well-organized, aggressive, and key performance indicator driven call center looks like. This video features me leading the call center at www.DJConnection.com back when I owned the business. You can also click the link below to visit the video as well if you are reading the e-book version of this book:

https://www.youtube.com/watch?v=oE7mEyChVDs&feature=emb_logo

WHEN MANAGING A SALES TEAM, YOU MUST REMEMBER THAT YOU SHOULD ONLY EXPECT WHATEVER YOU ACCEPT

If you allow your team to make only 50 calls per day that is what they are going to do by default. However, if you demand that your team dials and smiles and makes 300 calls per day that is what they will do. It is up to you as the leader of your company to set the standard when it comes to the performance of your people.

HOW MANY CALLS CAN A HUMAN ACTUALLY SUSTAINABLY MAKE?

Currently our team has been asked by the cosmetic surgeon Dr. Bryan Whitlock to call his current and former patients to do quality control calls. Bryan wants us to gather objective client feedback so that he can learn how to better serve his patients and so that he can also gather objective Google reviews from his real current and former patients and he is paying our team to make calls for him 8 hours per day. Approximately how many calls do you think that our team is able to make on his behalf every day? 50 calls? 100 calls? 200 calls? 250 calls? My friend, our team is able to make 250 calls each and every day, during an 8 hour day.

How? Because we have one individual who is 100% dedicated to calling his current and former patients and they are following scripts that have been approved by him. Thus, there is no bureaucracy, procrastination, or sales representatives asking the boss, "What should I say? Who should I call? What should I be doing during the day?"

MINIMIZE THE DISTRACTIONS FOR YOUR TEAM SO THAT THEY CAN TAKE MASSIVE ACTION

Because we have a sales representative who has no other tasks on her to-do list and because she is a diligent person we are making more calls for Dr. Bryan Whitlock in a day than most sales representatives ever make during a month. You must work to do everything in your power to eliminate the distractions that will stand in the way of your sales team maximizing the value that they can bring to every hour.

TO MAXIMIZE THE EFFICIENCY OF YOUR CALL TEAM MAKE SURE THAT YOU TAKE THE FOLLOWING ACTION STEPS BEFORE EXPECTING THEM TO BECOME EFFICIENT COLD-CALLERS:

* Make sure that your sales representatives have easy-to-learn scripts and nothing that could possibly interrupt them during their workday.

* Role play and practice with your sales representatives until they can't get it wrong, not just until they get it right.

* Ban smartphones from your call center. Make sure that your sales representatives do not bring their smartphones (and the constant distractions that they bring) to work.

* Install a keystroke recorder like ActivTrak.com to ensure that your sales people are not wasting their day visiting websites that are unrelated to dialing and smiling your ideal and likely buyers.

* Change the settings on the sales representatives computer so that they only have access to websites that you want them having access to (not ESPN.com, FoxNews.com, CNN.com, Facebook, Instagram.com and sites unrelated to their job).

* Install ClarityVoice.com so that you record each and every phone call that comes into your organization.

* Install Nest.com cameras in your workplace so that you know that your team is woking 100% of the time that you are paying them to be working.

* Hire a manager who holds everybody accountable to staying on the phones during the workday.

* Set up a tracking sheet so that every sales representative has to transparently report how many calls they made each and every day.

* Schedule a weekly sales training meeting with your team where you actually take the time to listen to their calls and to train your staff based upon the quality or lack-there-of, of the calls.

* Schedule daily morning huddles with your sales team to fire them up and to follow-up on yesterday's performance and to set the expectations for today's performance.

IF YOU HAVE THE BEST SALES SCRIPTS IN THE WORLD AND YOU DO NOT HAVE THE ACTION ITEMS LISTED ABOVE KNOCKED OUT, YOUR SALES SYSTEM WILL NOT WORK.

CHAPTER 13

TRAINING GREAT SALESPEOPLE IS NOT AN EVENT, IT'S A PROCESS

Each and every Monday morning at 8:00 AM you will find me training the Elephant In The Room (www.EITRLounge.com) team on how to become the best men's grooming experience that we can possibly be. Why? Because by default, myself and our team would drift into mediocrity if we were not intentional about improving each and every week. Each and every Tuesday at 7:00 AM you will find me training all of the salespeople that work for me and with me (www.ClayStaires.com, www.EITRLounge.com, www.MakeYourLifeEpic.com, www.RedmondGrowth.com, etc.) about how to become the best salesperson they can possibly be.

WHY?

Because without being intentional my team would actually get worse each and every week rather than improving. It is my role and your role as a leader to be intentional about ensuring that your team is getting better by 2% each and every week.

CHAPTER 14

COMMIT TO TAKING YOUR COMMUNICATION SKILLS TO THE NEXT LEVEL

Having closed thousands and thousands of deals throughout the years, having coached thousands of business owners, and having owned several multi-million dollar companies, I can tell you from first-hand experience that most relationship altering "misunderstandings" and "miscommunications" occur when well-meaning people begin to unintentionally work on different levels of communication at the same time within a transaction. In the world of verbal communication I sincerely believe that there are four different levels that humans can communicate on and it is vitally important for you to ensure that you are on the same level of communication of your ideal and likely buyer at all times.

THE FIRST LEVEL
Light talk, small talk and meaningless rapport building – This can be best described as "chit chat."

THE SECOND LEVEL
This is the cathartic conversations that fill 99% of the conversations of two soccer moms talking to one another. During these conversations each participant is looking to share their feelings, their personal emotions and their opinions.

THE THIRD LEVEL
This is the type of conversation that you typically find successful business people engaging in. During these types of conversations important information is shared and exchanged. Transfer of knowledge is accomplished during these conversations.

THE FOURTH LEVEL
Very few people ever become good at this level of communication because it involves persuasion. In order to excel at this level of communication you must be able to actually change the opinions of others as a result of having mastered the skills involved with:

Rapport – You must learn to excel at building rapport and an instant connection with your ideal and likely buyers.

Needs – You must become skilled at finding the needs and problems that you can solve.

Benefits – You must become great at delivering benefits and solutions that you can provide while providing irrefutable facts, examples and testimonials to prove that you are 100% honest and correct. Provide your ideal and likely buyers with what they need to know to choose to buy from you but do not bore your potential buyers with too much information, features and data smog.

Call to Action – You must become a master of calling the other party to take action after you have proven your point and shown how you, your point of view, your product or service can actually solve problems for them.

Isolate Objections – You must become great at finding the objections presented by your ideal and likely buyers (no time, no need or no money) so that you successfully overcome these objections and win the deal.

Call to Action (Again) – After you have thoroughly isolated and solved the objections of your ideal and likely buyers you must become comfortable with again asking for the sale. Your entire objective and goals it to get the buyer to commit (to the next appointment, to signing the contract, to paying a deposit, etc.). You don't need 35 potential closes. You just need to script out and to develop a close that works. Your closing script must be simple, easy to understand and easily trainable to people who are not you.

CHAPTER 15

DETERMINE THE OTHER PROBLEMS THAT YOU CAN SOLVE FOR YOUR IDEAL AND LIKELY BUYERS THAT NOW BOTH LIKE AND TRUST YOU

Once you have invested both the time and money to earn the trust of your ideal and likely buyers, life is going to get better for you. However, before you start celebrating your successes with too much enthusiasm I would encourage you to invest the time needed to write down all of the problems that you could solve for your ideal and likely buyers if given the opportunity. It is vitally important that you invest the time needed to create a list of all of the "add-on" services and products that your company can provide to your clients whose respect and trust you have just earned. In fact, over the years I have consulted and worked with huge companies who rely heavily on the "add-ons" in order to both survive and thrive. As examples:

1. When I built my first multi-million dollar business, www. DJConnection.com, I was constantly able to refer local high-quality photographers to brides who were looking for a great photographer. Over time I was able to negotiate a few solid referral fees from high-quality photographers and over time I started to develop a massive income stream as a result of getting paid referral fees from the wedding vendors that I recommended to brides-to-be. However, this would not have happened if I would have not methodically, consistently and habitually focused on asking each and every bride after the point of sale if they were still in need of a wedding photographer?

2. When you visit www.Southwest.com you will quickly discover that Southwest Airlines also offers vacation packages and car rental packages and no longer just the ability to schedule and book your airline tickets. Why? Their consumers typically need to rent a car once they land in a city that Southwest Airlines flies them to. Thus, Southwest has proactively decided to get into the game of allowing you to book your airline tickets, your hotel, your rental car and your vacation packages all in one place. And do they make money as a result of doing so? Absolutely, 100% yes!

Right now while this idea is still hot and fresh in your mind I challenge you to take the time needed to list out the problems that you and your team have the ability to solve for your ideal and likely buyers. Over the years I have worked with countless companies that produce the vast majority of their profits as a direct result of doing this including:

* www.DrBreck.com
* www.DrZoellner.com
* www.OXIFresh.com
* www.ScoreBBall.com
* www.TipTopK9.com
* www.PMHOKC.com

What problems can you solve for your ideal and likely buyers?

_____

_____

_____

_____

SUCCESS IS ACHIEVED AS A RESULT OF SCALABLY OFFERING THE WORLD A SOLUTION TO ONE OF THEIR PROBLEMS IN EXCHANGE FOR THE MONEY THAT YOU DESIRE.

MUSKETS

DAGNABBIT! MY HORSE BROKE DOWN AGAIN!

YOUR BUSINESS EXISTS TO SOLVE PROBLEMS
FOR YOU AND YOUR CUSTOMERS.
- CLAY CLARK
FOUNDER OF THRIVE15

* Steve Jobs provided the world with computers that the average human could actually use.

* Henry Ford made it affordable for humans to travel freely throughout the country.

* Russell Simmons introduced the world to beats, rhythms, and rap music they had never heard of.

* Justin Timberlake entertains us and makes us laugh with his musical, comedic, and acting skills.

* Larry Page and Sergey Brin made it possible for us to quickly find the answers to our problems by just typing something into a search bar.

* Andrew Carnegie teamed up with Henry Bessemer to make the manufacturing of steel efficient and affordable.

* Dr. Zoellner provides Tulsa with affordable eye glasses, contacts, and eye care.

* I, Clay Clark, made quality wedding entertainment both consistent and affordable.

* You, _____(your name), will provide _____ (solution, service, product, what?) in exchange for _____ (the riches that you seek?).

"GREAT SPIRITS HAVE ALWAYS ENCOUNTERED VIOLENT OPPOSITION FROM MEDIOCRE MINDS."
– ALBERT EINSTEIN
DEVELOPER OF THE GENERAL THEORY OF RELATIVITY

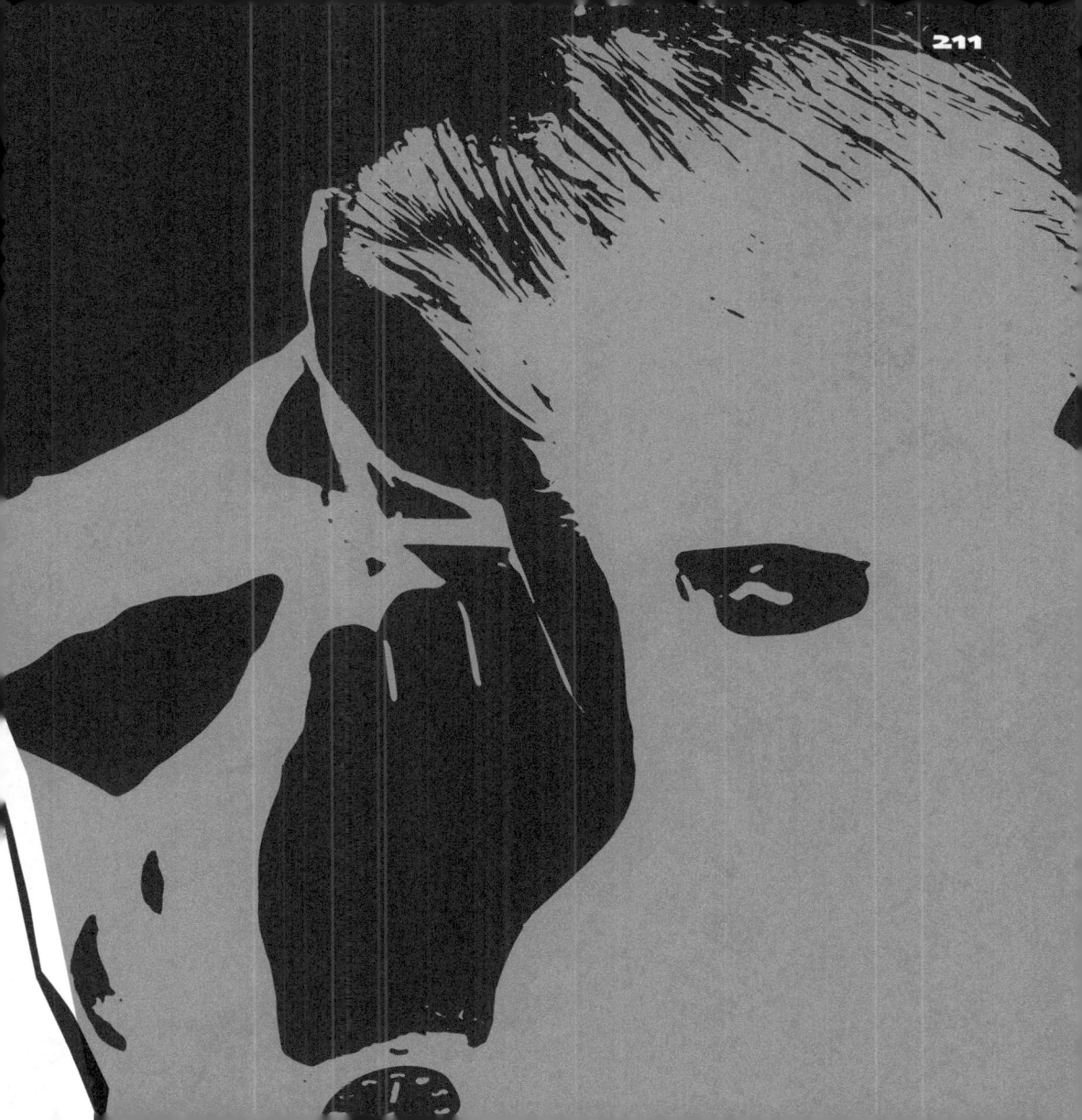

CHAPTER 16

HOW TO PROPERLY PRICE YOUR PRODUCTS AND SERVICES

Sooner than later you must learn how to become a "spectacular oddity" as opposed to competing in the world of commerce as a commodity because business owners and salespeople that live by discounting their prices also die by discounting their prices. Unless you are Wal-Mart or Amazon.com, I would strongly encourage you to not attempt to sustainably compete on price. Thus, you must design and create a memorable customer experience that wows each and everyone of your ideal and likely buyers in a way that your consumers would consider to be "spectacular."

* DEFINITION

Spectacular – Beautiful in a dramatic and eye-catching way.

* DEFINITION

Commodity – A raw material or primary agricultural product that can be bought and sold such as a copper or coffee.

* DEFINITION

Oddity – A strange or peculiar person, thing or trait.

In today's world, in the absence of value, price is the only consideration that a customer has. Again, "in the absence of value, price is the only consideration." Don't over spiritualize this or make this weird, but you must absolutely invest the time this week to mystery shop your competition. Yes, that's right. You must invest the time to discover what services and products that your competitors are offering and at what price they are offering their goods and services. As a business owner, you must know what you are competing against. In fact, you must know the following things about your competitors (at a minimum):

1. What services do your competitors offer?

2. What are your competitors charging for the services and products they provide?

3. What competitors offer a better product or service than you offer and why?

4. Do the websites of your competitors look better than yours and if so why?

5. How do your competitors answer their phones?

6. What pre-written emails do your competitors send to their lead inquiries?

CHAPTER 17

DECLARE WAR ON THE SALES-KILLING JARGON

By default, salespeople, professionals and academics love to use sales killing jargon at all-times to demonstrate their industry knowledge; however it kills rapport and it kills potential sales. If you want to sell more anytime soon, stop using jargon. I know that nerds, doctors, politicians and lawyers love to use jargon, but don't use jargon if you want your sales to increase. I'm not sure if salesmen think that jargon makes them sound smart, however I can tell you that the people who dislike the use of industry jargon and abbreviations more than anyone else, are your potential buyers.

Using jargon consistently on your potential buyers is a great way for you to demonstrate that you know a bunch about your industry, but it really does irritate your ideal and likely buyers. They don't know what you are talking about and you know that they don't know what you are talking about when you start using all of those abbreviations; so just stop with the jack-assery and start using words that other humans on the planet who are not industry insiders can understand (your ideal and likely buyers).

You must understand and remember that words which are not clearly understood by a 13-year-old are not going to be understood by your ideal and likely buyer adults either. Jargon does not help your cause. It hinders it. As you build your sales systems you must remember that co-founder of Apple, the former CEO of PIXAR, and founder of NeXT, Steve Jobs was correct when he once wrote, "Simplicity is the ultimate sophistication."

Stop killing your potential deals and your relationships with your ideal and likely buyers by speaking to them using exotic words that they don't understand and that you barely understand. Using acronyms, insider jargon and complex vocabulary truly is an impediment to your ability to sell well. In fact, on this very subject, this email was sent out by Elon Musk to stop the use of acronyms at SpaceX.

SUBJECT LINE:

ACRONYMS SERIOUSLY SUCK:

"There is a creeping tendency to use made up acronyms at SpaceX. Excessive use of made up acronyms is a significant impediment to communication and keeping communication good as we grow is incredibly important. Individually, a few acronyms here and there may not seem so bad, but if a thousand people are making these up, over time the result will be a huge glossary that we have to issue to new employees. No one can actually remember all these acronyms and people don't want to seem dumb in a meeting, so they just sit there in ignorance. This is particularly tough on new employees.

That needs to stop immediately or I will take drastic action - I have given enough warning over the years. Unless an acronym is approved by me, it should not enter the SpaceX glossary. If there is an existing acronym that cannot reasonably be justified, it should be eliminated, as I have requested in the past.

For example, there should be not "HTS" [horizontal test stand] or "VTS" [vertical test stand] designations for test stands. Those are particularly dumb, as they contain unnecessary words. A "stand" at our test site is obviously a test stand. VTS-3 is four syllables compared with "Tripod", which is two, so the bloody acronym version actually takes longer to say than the name!"

CHAPTER 18

A CONVERSATION ABOUT LIFE BEYOND JUST MOTIVATION

SALES PEOPLE LOVE TO READ MOTIVATIONAL BOOKS

and when they finish reading these notable, quotable, and inspiring books they feel like they can conquer the world, slay giants and gain new clients starting first thing tomorrow morning. When sales people read motivational books, they love it because it causes them to feel as though they can do anything, be anything and sell anything to anybody. However, having a burning desire to sell well is very different from actually having the skill, the scripts and the proven strategies needed to sell well. This is the equivalent of having the desire to play linebacker in the National Football League without having the 6 foot 3 inch and 238 pound body with the incredible speed, coordination, and understanding of the game to compete and actually play well in the National Football League.

My friend, your burning desire to become a persuasive person is not the same thing as actually being a persuasive person. Being highly motivated is simply an emotion where as being able to sell well involves learning a skill that is learnable and scalable. The vast majority of salespeople have bought the motivational audio trainings and have attended enough motivational seminars to the point that the average salesperson now actually believes that if you simply have that burning desire you can do whatever is required. However, if you have not taken the time to master the sales moves that I am teaching you throughout the pages of this book you simply cannot win regardless of how motivated you are.

DO WHAT YOU SAY YOU ARE GOING TO DO AND FOLLOW-THROUGH

In the world of sales, too many people rely on their relationships to cover up the fact that they have terrible communication skills and that they consistently fail to deliver on their promises. If you want to win and win big over the long haul, it is vitally important that you don't lie about and misrepresent what your products and services actually have the capacity to do for your ideal and likely buyers. In order to build the type of solid reputation that will lead to an increase in your compensation, you must do what you say you are going to do and more.

You must OBSESS about giving your clients more than they pay for each and every month that you have the honor to serve them. In order to become super successful you must BE ON TIME, ON BUDGET and your must ACCURATELY DELIVER ON WHAT YOU PROMISE.

In the world of sales you must treat each and every one of your clients as though they are people whom your life and livelihood depends on, because that is what they are. As an employee, I too would advise you to treat every interaction with your boss as though your financial success depends upon it, because it does.

MOTIVATED
TO MOTIVATE!

CHAPTER 19

DON'T COMPLICATE THE STRATEGY: CALL THEM ALL UNTIL THEY CRY, BUY OR DIE

COMPANIES THAT TRY TO CONTACT POTENTIAL CUSTOMERS WITHIN AN HOUR OF RECEIVING QUERIES ARE NEARLY **7X** **AS LIKELY TO HAVE MEANINGFUL CONVERSATIONS WITH KEY DECISION MAKERS AS FIRMS THAT TRY TO CONTACT PROSPECTS EVEN AN HOUR LATER.**

YET ONLY 37% OF COMPANIES RESPOND TO QUERIES WITHIN AN HOUR.

- HUBSPOT
$270 MILLION MARKETING & SALES COMPANY FOUNDED IN 2006

ANYWHERE FROM 35% TO 64% OF LEADS NEVER GET CALLED AT ALL.
- FORBES

ACCORDING TO A STUDY BY MARKETING DONUT, 80 PERCENT OF SALES TAKE 5 FOLLOW-UP PHONE CALLS AFTER THE INITIAL MEETING TO CLOSE.

01 02 03 04 05

HOWEVER, IT WAS FOUND IN THIS STUDY THAT **ALMOST HALF** OF SALESPEOPLE GIVE UP AFTER JUST ONE FOLLOW-UP.

CALL YOUR LEADS

TIMING IS EVERYTHING

50% OF SALES GO TO THE FIRST SALESPERSON TO CONTACT THE PROSPECT.
-INSIDESALES.COM
NET WORTH OVER $1 BILLION ACCORDING TO BUSINESS INSIDER

ONLY 27% OF LEADS EVER GET CONTACTED
-FORBES

27%

AN INCREASE FROM 27% TO 92% IS AN INCREASE OF 341% LIFT IN RESULTS JUST BY RESPONDING IMMEDIATELY AND PERSISTENTLY TO LEADS
- FORBES

RESPONDING IMMEDIATELY

341% LIFT

92%

27%

PERCENTAGE OF LEADS CONTACTED

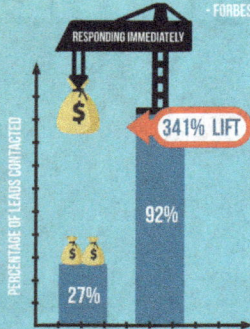

76% OF PEOPLE WHO CONDUCT A LOCAL SEARCH ON THEIR SMARTPHONE VISIT A BUSINESS WITHIN 24 HOURS

28% OF THOSE SEARCHES RESULT IN A PURCHASE

HUBSPOT
$270 MILLION MARKETING & SALES COMPANY FOUNDED IN 2006

A Clay Clark Creation

CHAPTER 20

THE DREAM 100 SYSTEM CAN AND WILL CHANGE YOUR LIFE!

THE "DREAM 100" IS A SYSTEM ORIGINALLY CREATED BY THE BEST-SELLING AUTHOR AND LEGENDARY SALES COACH, CHET HOLMES.

In this best-selling book, *The Ultimate Sales Machine*, Chet Holmes writes, "Best buyers buy more, buy faster, and buy more often than other buyers. These are your ideal clients. Have a special effort dedicated to just the dream clients."

I couldn't agree more. If you want to supercharge your sales and truly expand your opportunities for massive growth you owe it to yourself to invest the time needed to make a list of the DREAM accounts, the DREAM connections and the DREAM influencers who would absolutely have the power to change your life if they simply decided to buy your products and services, endorsed your products and services or were willing to partner with you in some way. Invest the time needed to create a "Dream 100" list and then methodically call, text, email and mail all of them until they cry, buy, or die. I would personally recommend that you would reach out to each of your "Dream 100 Targets" once per month.

NOTABLE QUOTABLE

"About 3 percent of potential buyers at any given time are buying now. 7 percent of the population is open to the idea of buying. The remaining 90 percent fall into one of three equal categories. The top third are "not thinking about it." The next third are "think they're not interested." The final third are "definitely not interested."

- CHET HOLMES
(THE BEST-SELLING AUTHOR OF *THE ULTIMATE SALES MACHINE* AND THE MAN WHO WAS ONCE THE BUSINESS PARTNER OF CHARLIE MUNGER)

As a result of diligently pursuing my Dream 100 list for our ThrivetimeShow.com podcast over the past 7 years we have been able to book the following big-time guests and more:

* Former CEO of YUM Brands (Pizza Hut, KFC, Taco Bell), David Novak

* Legendary Former Key Apple Employee Turned Venture Capitalist, Best Selling Author, Guy Kawasaki

* Senior pastor of the largest church in America with over 100,000 weekly attendees (Lifechurch.tv), Craig Groeschel

* 8x *New York Times* Best-Selling Author and Leadership Expert, John Maxwell

* Best-selling author and Pastor, John Bevere

* Celebrity Chef, Entrepreneur, and *New York Times* Best-Selling Author, Wolfgang Puck

* NBA Hall of Famer, David Robinson (2-time NBA Champion, 2-time Gold Medal Winner)

* *New York Times* Best-Selling Co-Author of *Rich Dad Poor Dad*, Sharon Lechter

* One of America's most trusted financial experts and has written nine consecutive *New York Times* bestsellers with 7 million+ books in print, David Bach

* Senior Editor for *Forbes* and 3x Best-Selling Author, Zack O'Malley Greenburg

* Most Downloaded Business Podcaster of All-Time (EOFire.com), John Lee Dumas

* *New York Times* Best-Selling Author of *Purple Cow*, and former Yahoo! Vice President of Marketing, Seth Godin

* Co-Founder of the 700+ Employee Advertising Company (AdRoll), Adam Berke

* Emmy Award-winning Producer of the Today Show and *New York Times* Best-Selling Author of *Sh*tty Moms*, Mary Ann Zoellner

* *New York Times* Best-Selling Author of *Contagious: Why Things Catch On* and Wharton Business Professor, Jonah Berger

* *New York Times* Best-Selling Author of *Made to Stick* and Duke University Professor, Dan Heath

* International Best-Selling Author of *In Search of Excellence*, Tom Peters

* NBA Player and Coach, Muggsy Bogues (Shortest player to ever play in the league)

* NFL Running Back, Rashad Jennings (and Winner of Dancing with the Stars)

* Lee Cockerell (The former Executive Vice President of Walt Disney World who once managed 40,000 employees)

* Michael Levine (PR consultant of choice for Michael Jackson, Prince, Nike, Charlton Heston, Nancy Kerrigan, etc.)

* Billboard Contemporary Christian Top 40 Recording Artist, Colton Dixon

* Conservative Talk Pundint, Frequent Fox News Contributor, Political Commentator and Best-Selling Author, Ben Shapiro

* See additional guests at Thrivetimeshow.com

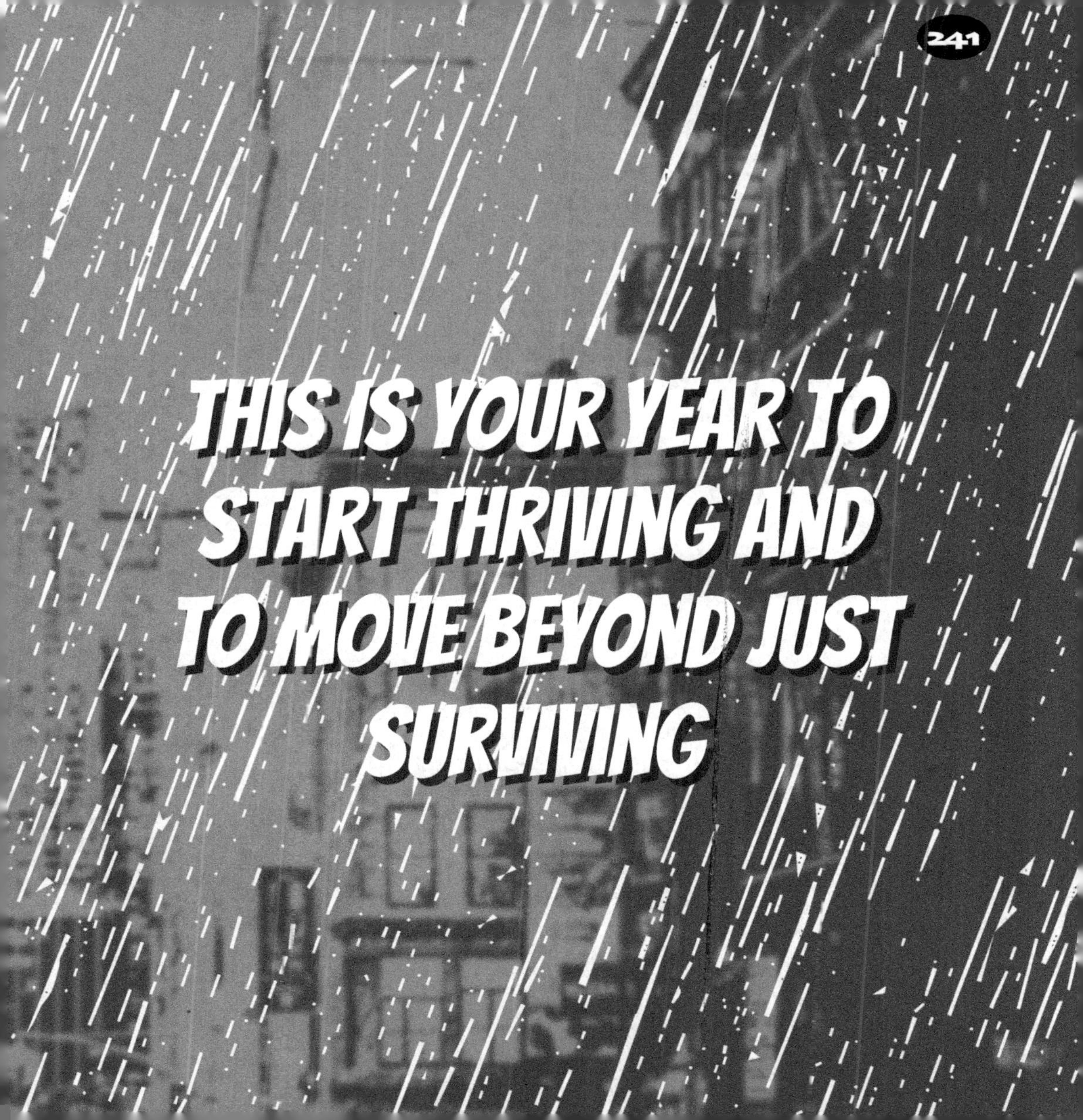
THIS IS YOUR YEAR TO START THRIVING AND TO MOVE BEYOND JUST SURVIVING

Although this book isn't going to teach you everything that you'll ever need to know about sales, I strongly believe that this book is going to change your life if you will simply take the time to apply the principles, strategies, systems and scripts found within the book. If you want to truly learn as much as possible about sales, I would highly recommend that you would invest the time needed to read the following books until you have mastered your craft:

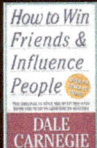

How to Win Friends and Influence People
BY DALE CARNEGIE

Soft Selling in a Hard World
BY JERRY VASS

The New Conceptual Selling: The Most Effective and Proven Method for Face-to-Face Sales Planning
BY ROBERT MILLER AND STEPHEN HEIMAN

The Ultimate Sales Machine
BY CHET HOLMES

My highest and most sincere desire is to help you to create both time and financial freedom so that you can live a life like I now do. I now work because I want to; and with only the 160 clients that I want to work with. I can now travel where I want and when I want, and I can now choose to spend my time however I want to. Thus, I chose to invest my time with YOU and into YOU because I know that once you too learn how to sell, a world of opportunities awaits you. If you feel stuck in any way, shape, or form, please do not hesitate to contact us or to attend one of our 2-Day in-person Thrivetime Show workshops.

Learn more at www.ThrivetimeShow.com/conferences.

WANT TO KNOW EVEN MORE?

Check out all of Clay's books

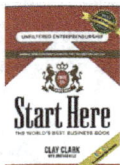

START HERE
The World's Best Business Growth & Consulting Book: Business Growth Strategies from the World's Best Business Coach.

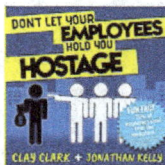

DON'T LET YOUR EMPLOYEES HOLD YOU HOSTAGE
This candid book shares how to avoid being held hostage by employees.

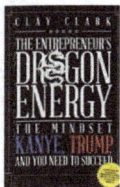

THE ENTREPRENEUR'S DRAGON ENERGY
The Mindset Kanye, Trump and You Need to Succeed.

TRADE-UPS
Learn how to design and live the life you love, how to find and create the time needed to get things done in a world filled with endless digital distractions, and more!

JACKASSARY
Jackassery will serve as a beacon of light for other entrepreneurs that are looking to avoid troublesome employees and difficult situations. This is real. This is raw. This is unfiltered entrepreneurship.

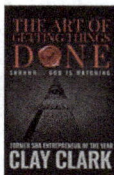

THE ART OF GETTING THINGS DONE
Clay Clark breaks down the proven, time-tested and time freedom creating super moves that you can use to create both the time freedom and financial freedom that most people only dream about.

THRIVE
How to Take Control of Your Destiny and Move Beyond Surviving... Now!

MANAGEMENT IS MENTORSHIP
9 Big Ideas for Effectively Managing Your Business in an Increasingly Dumb, Distracted & Dishonest America

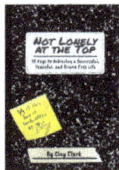

IT'S NOT LONELY AT THE TOP

15 Keys to achieving a successful, peaceful, and drama-free life.

(3/4 of this book is handwritten by Clay Clark, himself)

SEARCH ENGINE DOMINATION

Learn the Proven System We've Used to Earn Millions.

F6 JOURNAL

Meta Thrive Time Journal.

MAKE YOUR LIFE EPIC

Clay shares his journey and struggle from the dorm room to the board room during his raw and action-packed story of how he built DJConnection.com.

PODCAST DOMINATION 101

This book will show you how to prepare, record, luanc, and begin generating income from your podcast, all from your home studio!

HOW TO REPEL FRIENDS AND NOT INFLUENCE PEOPLE

The epic whale of a tale featuring America's self proclaimed most humble male

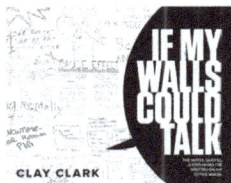

IF MY WALLS COULD TALK

The Notes, Quotes, & Epiphanies I've Written On Clay's Office Walls. (Hardcover)

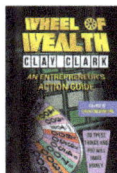

WHEEL OF WEALTH

An Entrepreneur's Action Guide.

BOOM

The 14 Proven Steps to Business Success.

CPSIA information can be obtained
at www.ICGtesting.com
Printed in the USA
BVHW061941200521
607796BV00002B/78

9 781734 229691